SCHIZOPHRENIA
WHEN REALITY BECOMES DISTORTED

By Michelle Harris

LUCENT
PRESS

D1291924

Published in 2019 by
Lucent Press, an Imprint of Greenhaven Publishing, LLC
353 3rd Avenue
Suite 255
New York, NY 10010

Designer: Andrea Davison-Bartolotta
Editor: Jennifer Lombardo

Library of Congress Cataloging-in-Publication Data

Names: Harris, Michelle, 1986- author.
Title: Schizophrenia : when reality becomes distorted / Michelle Harris.
Description: New York : Lucent Press, 2019. | Series: Diseases and disorders | Includes bibliographical references and index.
Identifiers: LCCN 2018032688 (print) | LCCN 2018035129 (ebook) | ISBN 9781534564961 (eBook) | ISBN 9781534564954 (library bound book) | ISBN 9781534564947 (pbk. book)
Subjects: LCSH: Schizophrenia. | Schizophrenia–Treatment. | Mental illness.
Classification: LCC RC514 (ebook) | LCC RC514 .H332 2019 (print) | DDC 616.89/8–dc23
LC record available at https://lccn.loc.gov/2018032688

Printed in the United States of America

CPSIA compliance information: Batch #BW19KL: For further information contact Greenhaven Publishing LLC, New York, New York at 1-844-317-7404.

Please visit our website, www.greenhavenpublishing.com. For a free color catalog of all our high-quality books, call toll free 1-844-317-7404 or fax 1-844-317-7405.

CONTENTS

Illness is an unfortunate part of life, and it is one that is often misunderstood. Thanks to advances in science and technology, people have been aware for many years that diseases such as the flu, pneumonia, and chicken pox are caused by viruses and bacteria. These diseases all cause physical symptoms that people can see and understand, and many people have dealt with these diseases themselves. However, sometimes diseases that were previously unknown in most of the world turn into epidemics and spread across the globe. Without an awareness of the method by which these diseases are spread—through the air, through human waste or fluids, through sexual contact, or by some other method—people cannot take the proper precautions to prevent further contamination. Panic often accompanies epidemics as a result of this lack of knowledge.

Knowledge is power in the case of mental disorders, as well. Mental disorders are just as common as physical disorders, but due to a lack of awareness among the general public, they are often stigmatized. Scientists have studied them for years and have found that they are generally caused by hormonal imbalances in the brain, but they have not yet determined with certainty what causes those imbalances or how to fix them. Because even mild mental illness is stigmatized in Western society, many people prefer not to talk about it.

Chronic pain disorders are also not well understood—even by researchers—and do not yet have foolproof treatments. People who have a mental disorder or a disease or disorder that causes them to feel chronic pain can be the target of uninformed opinions. People who do not have these disorders sometimes struggle to understand how difficult it can be to deal with the symptoms. These disorders are often termed "invisible illnesses" because no one can see the symptoms; this leads many people to doubt that they exist or are serious problems. Additionally, people who have an undiagnosed disorder may understand that they are experiencing the world in a different way than their peers, but they have no one to turn to for answers.

Misinformation about all kinds of ailments is often spread through personal anecdotes, social media, and even news sources. This series aims to present accurate information about both physical and mental conditions so young adults will have a better understanding of them. Each volume discusses the symptoms of a particular disease or disorder, ways it is currently being treated, and the research that is being done to understand it further. Advice for people who may be suffering from a disorder is included, as well as information for their loved ones about how best to support them.

With fully cited quotes, a list of recommended books and websites for further research, and informational charts, this series provides young adults with a factual introduction to common illnesses. By learning more about these ailments, they will be better able to prevent the spread of contagious diseases, show compassion to people who are dealing with invisible illnesses, and take charge of their own health.

WHAT IS SCHIZOPHRENIA?

Mental illness, much like physical illness, can leave a person feeling not quite themselves. Symptoms can arise so slowly that it may take a while before they realize something is wrong. They might chalk it up to outside influences, such as long hours spent studying before exams, a recent breakup, or drama with friends. Unlike many physical ailments, however, mental illness brings with it a stigma, or negative view, that can make people hesitant or completely unwilling to seek help. They may brush off their symptoms by saying something such as "I'm fine," or underestimate the severity of their illness by saying something such as, "It's not a big deal. I can handle it." Unfortunately, the longer a person waits to seek treatment for any illness—physical or mental—the worse things get. The mental disorder schizophrenia has a particularly

One of the things schizophrenia affects is the way people feel and show emotion.

6

negative stigma and can become especially difficult for individuals to handle without professional help.

Schizophrenia is a mental illness that affects the way a person perceives reality, making it hard for them to tell the difference between what is real and what is imaginary. They often also have difficulty expressing emotions the way other people do, which may make them seem to be acting inappropriately in social situations. This disorder can cause a range of different issues, which can impact the person's daily functioning and well-being. Although schizophrenia can lead to severe changes in an individual's personality and functioning when it is left untreated, the disorder is not a light switch that suddenly flicks on one day. Rather, symptoms develop slowly—a small flicker, hardly noticeable at first, which gradually builds up. A teen used to falling asleep the second their head hits the pillow may start to struggle to quiet their thoughts, relax, and drift off. A clear request to take out the trash may take a few seconds to process, as if several people had spoken at once, making the request difficult to understand. A student may start struggling to complete a major paper, finding it difficult to sift through the fog in their head to focus on the task. Eventually, these symptoms multiply and begin to grow more severe, making it difficult for the person to figure out what is real and what is just happening in their mind.

Throughout history, people suffering from mental illness have been treated extremely poorly. From neglect and isolation to outright physical and emotional abuse, the road to humane treatment for those with mental illness has been a bumpy one. This painful history, as well as misinformation and the harsh stigma attached to mental illness, has created challenges patients and care providers alike face daily.

Schizophrenia in the Media

A major contributor to the stigma surrounding mental illness in general—and schizophrenia in particular—is the media and how it portrays individuals with mental disorders. Despite research showing that people with mental illness are far more likely to be victims of violent crime than perpetrators of it, movies and television shows consistently depict characters with mental illness as violent criminals. A study published in 2012 showed that more than 80 percent of characters with schizophrenia in films were depicted as violent, and approximately one-third engaged in homicidal behavior. Additionally, many villains in horror movies have some sort of mental illness that either is never identified or includes symptoms many mentally ill people do not experience in real life.

In the *Halloween* films, the main antagonist is Michael Myers (shown here), a man who escapes from the sanitarium where he was receiving psychiatric care and murders several people.

The slasher film series *Halloween* is a classic example of the horror trope of the psychiatric patient with an unspecified mental illness who becomes a homicidal maniac. Another is Jack Nicholson's character in the 1980 film *The Shining*, which is based on the book of the same name by Stephen King. Nicholson's character, Jack Torrance, is a writer who experiences mood swings, nightmares, and vivid hallucinations, which ultimately lead to a violent spree. A third is the classic 1960 horror movie *Psycho*, in which Norman Bates, a young man who presumably has dissociative identity disorder (DID), murders multiple people while presenting as his mother. In a more recent film, 2016's *Split* with James McAvoy, a man with DID kidnaps and kills several people, and one of his personalities unrealistically gives him superhuman abilities. In response to this movie, the International Society for the Study of Trauma and Dissociation (ISSTD) issued a statement criticizing the way the movie "acts to further marginalize those who already struggle on a daily basis with the weight of stigma."[1] The statement also said,

> *The 1000 plus therapists and practitioners in the International Society for the Study of Trauma and Dissociation (ISSTD) and the tens of thousands across the world who treat complex trauma and dissociative disorders understand the desire to make entertaining movies that make money. We would ask that this not be done at the expense of a vulnerable population that struggles to be recognized and receive the effective treatment that they deserve.[2]*

In reality, experts have said, people with mental illness are more likely to be violent toward themselves than toward others. For example, studies show that rates of suicide and self-harm are higher among people with schizophrenia.

Not all film portrayals of mental illness are negative, however. In 1993's *Benny and Joon*, a young woman with schizophrenia named Joon falls in love with a quirky young man named Sam, much to the disappointment of Joon's brother Benny, who has devoted his life to caring for her to keep her out of an institution. The film depicts the hallucinations Joon hears and how consistent routine and regular medication help her keep her symptoms under control.

Importantly, it also shows that a person with schizophrenia can still find love and live independently if they have the right support.

In the movie *Benny and Joon*, Joon (left) falls in love with Sam (center), showing that people with schizophrenia can have normal romantic relationships.

In 1991's *The Fisher King*, actor Robin Williams portrays Parry, a homeless man who believes he is on a quest for the Holy Grail. Eventually, it is revealed that his real name is Harry Sagan and he is a former teacher who fell into a catatonic state after witnessing the murder of his wife. A catatonic state, also called catatonia, is when a person does not move or speak even though there is nothing wrong with their body. Catatonia can also describe abnormal movements. Parry experiences auditory hallucinations and falls into catatonia again when he is attacked on the street. In addition to depicting multiple symptoms of schizophrenia, the film shows how stressful life events can trigger psychosis.

Common Myths and Misconceptions

When hearing the word "schizophrenia," a number of different images may come to mind. Due mainly to varying depictions in the media, which often confuse schizophrenia with psychopathy, many people have a frightened reaction to the word. Psychopathy is not one symptom, but several. Someone who exhibits psychopathy is manipulative and cruel to others, does not feel guilt for hurting other people either physically or emotionally, lies whenever it benefits them, and has a hard time exercising self-control.

In an article on the website Vice, a man who chose to identify himself as Daniel Smith to protect his privacy wrote,

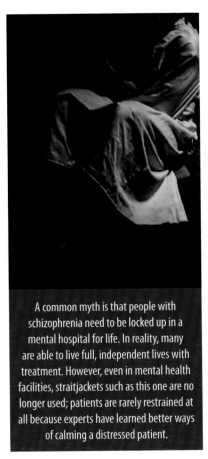

A common myth is that people with schizophrenia need to be locked up in a mental hospital for life. In reality, many are able to live full, independent lives with treatment. However, even in mental health facilities, straitjackets such as this one are no longer used; patients are rarely restrained at all because experts have learned better ways of calming a distressed patient.

until I became schizophrenic, the word represented a death sentence in my mind. When you hear of people being schizophrenic, you imagine them locked in rooms with padded walls, rocking backwards and forwards into a two-dimensional future of heavily medicated conversations and drool-covered pillows. You imagine a future of hearing voices and seeing phantoms. This is far from the case if it's treated well. With the right treatment, and especially if it's caught early, you can recover incredibly well from acute schizophrenia, as you can from other mental illnesses.[3]

Additionally, schizophrenia is often confused for other mental illnesses. Some of the most popular misconceptions about schizophrenia are that it results in "split" or multiple personalities, it makes a person violent and dangerous, it results from bad parenting, and sufferers can never recover and need to live out their days in a mental hospital. However, none of this is true. A person who displays multiple personalities is likely suffering from DID rather than schizophrenia, and while the crazed killer in a television show or movie may be described as schizophrenic, most real people with the disorder are nonviolent, especially if they are receiving treatment. Having schizophrenia also does not mean that a person is "insane." Insanity is a legal term used to describe someone who is too mentally ill to be held responsible for a crime; it is not a word used in medicine. Typically, a person experiencing psychosis is not legally insane and generally does not commit crimes. The word "crazy" is also not used in a medical context, and mental illness advocates such as Lydia X. Z. Brown say that using it casually (such as, "He just went crazy" to talk about someone who lost their temper) or to refer to people who have a legitimate mental illness "sends the message that it's OK to trivialize mental illness and lazily substitute real people's lived experiences for 'wild,' 'silly,' 'dangerous,' or 'out of control.'"[4]

People with schizophrenia are not crazy; they have a treatable mental illness. Although it is true that there is currently no cure for schizophrenia, advancements in treatment—including medication, rehabilitation, and psychosocial therapies—can help people lead active, independent, and fulfilling lives. It is not an easy condition to cope with, but mental health experts as well as schizophrenia patients say it is not impossible either. Historically, people with mental illness often were not treated with kindness, compassion, or empathy. Currently, mental health advocates say society could still do a lot more for its members who are struggling. However, the improvements that have been made over the last century are vast, meaningful, and continuing. As Smith wrote, "Mental illness is no different from physical illness—it just involves a different organ: the brain."[5]

CHAPTER ONE

A "MAD" HISTORY

Tracing the history of schizophrenia is difficult, as it was lumped into the generic term of "madness," along with a number of other mental disorders, for centuries. It was not until the early 1900s that doctors began to distinguish the disorder from other illnesses. Schizophrenia was first described in 1899 by German psychiatrist Dr. Emil Kraepelin. In the sixth edition of his textbook, *Compendium der Psychiatrie*, Dr. Kraepelin named the disorder "dementia praecox," or premature dementia. Through his analysis of a large number of cases, Kraepelin determined that though the patients he was treating had a different variety of symptoms, the similar progression of their illnesses meant that they were all experiencing the same disorder. Later, in 1908, Swiss psychiatrist Eugen Bleuler coined the term schizophrenia, a combination of Greek words meaning "split mind." This term may have contributed to the confusion between schizophrenia and DID, but Bleuler did not mean that people with schizophrenia have multiple personalities. What he actually meant was a split between thoughts and emotions as well as a withdrawal from reality.

Dr. Emil Kraepelin coined the term "dementia praecox" in 1899 to describe the disorder that would later be called schizophrenia.

Historical accounts of people displaying signs now recognized as symptoms of schizophrenia have been found from as far back as 2000 BC. "Madness" was believed to have divine origins. Some considered it a gift from the gods to inspire artists, while others believed it to be a sign of demonic possession. Greek physician Hippocrates, who lived from about 460 to 375 BC, introduced a more down-to-earth—but ultimately false—theory, hypothesizing that madness was caused by an imbalance of the four bodily "humours" (blood, phlegm, and black and yellow biles). Treatment therefore focused on restoring balance to the humours, which doctors of the time believed could be done through lifestyle and dietary changes, bloodletting (draining blood from the patient, often by cutting them or putting blood-sucking organisms called leeches on their body), purging (giving the patient things that would make them throw up or go to the bathroom frequently), and more. The Romans, according to the website History Cooperative, treated madness with "warm baths, massage and diets, although more punitive [punishing] treatments were also suggested by Cornelius Celsus, stemming from the belief that the symptoms were caused through having angered the gods, and included flogging [whipping] and starvation."[6] During the Middle Ages and Renaissance, witchcraft and demonic possession were believed to be the cause of severe mental illness, so mentally ill people were treated with exorcism—a process that was believed to make demons leave a person's body—and torture.

For centuries, individuals with a mental illness were kept locked away from society for their own safety and the safety of others. Until the establishment of mental institutions, family members and loved ones were responsible for these "mad" people. If this was not an option, individuals were left to fend for themselves on the streets. In the Middle Ages, a few Christian groups began creating asylums to house and care for the mentally ill. Bedlam in London, England, was the first and most infamous.

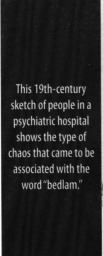
This 19th-century sketch of people in a psychiatric hospital shows the type of chaos that came to be associated with the word "bedlam."

Bedlam was first established in 1247 as the Priory of St. Mary of Bethlehem. The name was shortened to Bethlem, which people later started pronouncing as "Bedlam." In 1547, the asylum came under control of the City of London and was the only public mental institution in England until the 1800s. Although Bedlam was created with the honorable intentions of caring for the homeless and ill, it became notorious for the cruel treatment of its patients, including beating, shackling, starving, hygienic neglect, and even murder. According to Ron Powers, author of the book *No One Cares About Crazy People*, "The poor, uneducated, and embittered jailers [at Bedlam] unleashed levels and varieties of cruelty both physical and psychological upon their 'patients' that have not been surpassed in history."[7] Visitors would pay to view the "lunatics," as if they were animals in a zoo. According to the BBC, visiting the hospital was "meant to be an instructive

reminder to visitors to 'keep baser instincts in check'…
lest they, too, wind up on the other side of the bars."[8]
Today, the word "bedlam" is still used to describe a
disorderly, confusing situation.

Dorothea Dix and the Fight for Hospital Reform

Born in 1802 in Hampden, Massachusetts, Dorothea Dix was a social reformer and humanitarian who spent the bulk of her lifetime fighting for the rights of the mentally ill and pushing for legislation in multiple states to establish hospitals specifically for the care of the mentally ill. After returning from a two-year trip to England, Dix began touring hospitals and correctional facilities across the United States, documenting the inhumane conditions and treatment of the mentally ill patients. She then took her findings to lawmakers in the United States and Canada to urge them to create asylums, which could properly care for the mentally ill with the attention and compassion they deserve. Her work directly led to the establishment of 32 institutions and the restructuring of many hospitals in North America. When the Civil War broke out in the United States, Dix committed to the Union cause and became the Superintendent of Army Nurses for the Union Army, helping to advance the role of female nurses in the medical field. According to the National Women's History Museum, Dix personally appointed more than 3,000 of the Union Army nurses, which was about 15 percent of the total. She died on July 17, 1887, leaving behind a legacy of activism.

Dorothea Dix was an American activist who lobbied state and federal governments to establish hospitals specifically for humane care of the mentally ill.

It was not until the 1800s that the idea of "moral treatment" for the mentally ill became popular, resulting in a wave of reforms and the construction of numerous new hospitals throughout Europe and the United States. Introduced by William Tuke in the late 1700s, moral treatment turned away from the common treatments of the time—including blood-letting, purging, and physical restraints—in favor of a more discipline-based treatment that essentially treated patients much like children. Brought to Life, a website exploring the history of medicine that is run by the Science Museum of London, explained,

> *Patients were expected to dine at the table, make polite conversation over tea, consider the consequences of their actions, and clean and garden. The asylum director established comprehensive rules and constant surveillance, enforced by simple rewards and punishments. Sanity was to be restored through self-discipline.*[9]

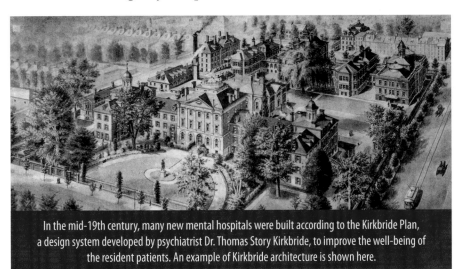

In the mid-19th century, many new mental hospitals were built according to the Kirkbride Plan, a design system developed by psychiatrist Dr. Thomas Story Kirkbride, to improve the well-being of the resident patients. An example of Kirkbride architecture is shown here.

Around the same time, French physician Philippe Pinel was also advocating for treating the mentally ill as patients rather than criminals. This shift in treatment, along with a boost in public funding, led to the creation of large, state-run hospitals. Many of these new facilities were designed according to Dr. Thomas Story Kirkbride's 1854 book, *On The Construction, Organization and General Arrangements Of Hospitals For The Insane*, which created a standardized blueprint for buildings that housed mentally ill patients. Mental hospitals that followed Kirkbride's design, which featured staggered wings to allow for streaming natural light and greater air ventilation, were typically located in isolated areas with beautiful gardens. Kirkbride felt this would allow patients to focus on recovery in a less stressful environment than a city. According to the website Living with Schizophrenia,

> *Sometimes these institutions were genuine places of sanctuary from the stresses of the world and benefited from compassionate and progressive leadership and provided a caring environment where people with schizophrenia could do well. Sadly, other institutions were less progressive where people with mental illness endured years of abusive treatment at the hands of sadistic [cruel] staff.*[10]

Unfortunately, even the nicest mental institutions could not provide quality care when they became overcrowded. Nearly 300 state hospitals were opened in the United States between 1845 and 1955, increasing the number of patients from roughly 2,000 to nearly 600,000. As public funding failed to keep up with the drastic increase in patient population and staff became overwhelmed, the focus shifted from providing care to maintaining order. Not unlike the asylums of the past, difficult patients were restrained and punished. Those whose mental illness had no cure, such as those with schizophrenia, were transferred to "back wards" where they were restrained with handcuffs or straitjackets and subjected to medical treatments such as lobotomization. Unsurprisingly, few patients improved under these conditions.

There is some debate over whether mental institutions of the past were cruel on purpose or by accident. It is likely that at least some of the past caretakers were deliberately cruel, since mentally ill people were often not viewed as "real" people who deserved to be treated kindly. According to Powers, institutions such as Bedlam often hired people from the lower classes of society to watch over psychiatric patients, which often gave them the feeling that they were better than the patients, leading them to abuse their power by being cruel. Others, however, believe many of the treatments that are now seen as inhumane were given to patients out of ignorance. Dr. Celia Spacone worked for 30 years at the Buffalo Psychiatric Center in Buffalo, New York. In a 2018 interview, she explained,

> *When you look at the history of some of the treatments that were used with people with mental illness, in retrospect now—they were not kind—they were not gentle and they were not helpful, yet I try to look at those things in light of what people's intentions were. Some of the things [we're] doing now to treat various disorders, they may find out 20, 30 years from [now that] we were completely wrong, but I think people did it with the best of intentions and that's what I try to hang on to— that notion. People did what they thought was the right thing.*[11]

Mental institutions were sometimes used as testing grounds for experimental treatments. Bedlam pioneered the use of medication to treat patients suffering from mental illness, including drugs such as opium and morphine, as well as tonics and laxatives. While these were not particularly effective antipsychotic medications, they were a start. The 20th century saw the rise of other treatments, including electroconvulsive therapy, or ECT (also known as electroshock therapy) and lobotomization. The idea of cutting into a person's skull to treat illness has been around for ages. For thousands of years, people around the world practiced trepanning, a crude surgical procedure that involved drilling holes in the skull to release the evil spirits people believed were trapped inside. While trepanation created holes in the skull, lobotomization took things a step further by then altering the brain inside.

A "Cutting Edge" Cure: Lobotomy

The first lobotomy was performed in 1935 by Portuguese neuropsychiatrist António Egas Moniz. The procedure involved drilling one hole into each side of the skull and inserting a sharp object, similar to an ice pick, into the brain to cut or destroy tissue. Moniz believed that cutting the connections between the neurons would stop the patient's abnormal thinking. A few years later, surgeon Walter J. Freeman II developed the more refined transorbital lobotomy, in which a needle was inserted in the brain through the eye socket and rotated to destroy the brain tissue. Seen as a "miracle cure" for a number of mental illnesses, including schizophrenia and depression, the procedure quickly became widespread. Dr. Moniz even won the Nobel Prize in 1949 for inventing the procedure. By the 1950s, the serious side effects of the procedure, including seizures, loss of motor coordination, partial paralysis, and very poor intellectual and emotional responsiveness, became more well-known, and public concern for civil rights grew. The discovery of effective antipsychotic drugs finally put an end to this treatment. More refined psychosurgical procedures are still used today, but only as a last resort and in very severe cases.

In the 1962 novel and 1975 film *One Flew Over the Cuckoo's Nest*, an unruly patient in a mental hospital is lobotomized so the staff can regain control over the institution. Shown here is actor Jack Nicholson, who played this character in the film.

The practice of using ECT began in Italy in the late 1930s. Psychiatry professor Dr. Ugo Cerletti and his assistant Lucio Bini selected patients with schizophrenia for their trials in which they applied electricity directly to the brain to induce seizures. The treatment proved successful and quickly caused a stir in the field of psychiatry. Prior to the invention of ECT, psychiatrists used chemicals to induce seizures, which were proven to be effective at relieving symptoms of mental illness. However, before the chemicals took effect, they caused the patient to experience a strong sense of fear, and there was no way the doctor could control the seizures once they started. This could be very dangerous; a drug called Metrazol created seizures that were so strong they caused spinal fractures in 42 percent of patients. ECT provided a less frightening and more controllable alternative. Although the early form of ECT was effective in reducing symptoms, it was still dangerous, resulting in memory loss and other serious complications, including broken bones. This was because patients were awake while undergoing ECT, so the seizure caused by the electric shock made their bodies thrash around.

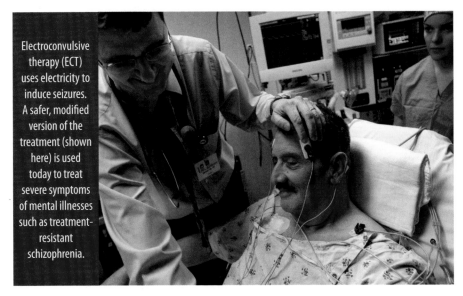

Electroconvulsive therapy (ECT) uses electricity to induce seizures. A safer, modified version of the treatment (shown here) is used today to treat severe symptoms of mental illnesses such as treatment-resistant schizophrenia.

Unfortunately, many institutions used ECT—and the threat of it—to control difficult patients and keep order in the wards rather than to treat symptoms, increasing the negative stigma associated with the treatment. Over time, the treatment has been modified and fine-tuned to decrease the danger to patients.

The treatment is much safer today—for example, patients are now put to sleep with medication before the treatment. Because an unconscious body does not thrash during a seizure, there is no longer a danger of breaking bones. ECT is now used to effectively treat severe symptoms of mental illnesses, including severe and treatment-resistant schizophrenia, depression, mania, catatonia, and dementia-related aggression. While it does still cause side effects, such as memory loss and headaches, they are mild compared to the side effects patients experienced in the past. Actress Carrie Fisher, known for her role as Leia in the *Star Wars* film franchise, was outspoken and candid about her history with bipolar disorder, detailing her experience with ECT in her 2008 memoir *Wishful Drinking* and in her 2011 memoir *Shockaholic*. "Some of my memories will never return. They are lost—along with the crippling feeling of defeat and hopelessness. Not a tremendous price to pay,"[12] she wrote in *Wishful Drinking*.

Schizophrenia and Eugenics

People most often associate eugenics (the idea that the human race can be "perfected" by controlled breeding) with the Nazis and their campaign for a master race. However, although Adolf Hitler and his regime took the idea to devastating and horrific ends, the eugenics movement did not actually begin in Germany. It was British scientist Sir Francis Galton, one of Charles Darwin's cousins, who coined the term "eugenics" in 1883. Galton had been analyzing the biographical information of several upper class English families when he concluded that certain qualities, such as high intelligence and special talents, were inherited. Therefore, he theorized, if all the smartest, most talented people produced more babies together, humanity as a whole could be improved. The idea became popular both in England and abroad.

Sir Francis Galton, an English scientist, coined the term "eugenics" in 1883.

However, while Galton's followers in England were focused on encouraging more "desirable" traits in society, eugenicists in the United States became more interested in weeding out the undesirable ones. One of many issues with eugenics is what to do about those traits society considers undesirable—and the people who have those qualities. In 1907, Indiana became the first state to pass a bill for the forced sterilization of people with mental disorders, as well as criminals and other so-called "defectives." Sterilization is the process of performing surgery to ensure that a person cannot have children. Several other states passed similar laws, which resulted in the sterilization of at least 45,000 Americans between 1907 and 1945, more than 20,000 of whom were patients in state mental hospitals.

When this type of law was passed in Virginia in 1924, the superintendant of a mental institution called the Virginia State Colony for Epileptics and Feebleminded wanted a case brought before the Supreme Court so no one would be able to later question whether the law was constitutional. In the 1927 case of *Buck v. Bell*, Virginia Colony officials argued that 17-year-old Carrie Buck should be sterilized because she and her mother, Emma Buck, "shared the hereditary traits of feeblemindedness and sexual promiscuity."[13]

Carrie was neither mentally ill, mentally challenged, nor sexually promiscuous; she had been sent to the Virginia Colony by her foster parents after becoming pregnant when a relative of her foster parents raped her. Sadly, it was not uncommon for mental institutions in the past to be used as a place where people could be sent on false pretenses if their family wanted to hide a secret, such as an unmarried mother. However, the court sided with the states in *Buck v. Bell.* Supreme Court Justice Oliver Wendell Holmes Jr. stated at the time, "It is better for all the world, if instead of waiting to execute degenerate offspring for crime, or to let them starve for their imbecility, society can prevent those who are manifestly unfit from continuing their kind."[14]

In the 1930s, the Nazi regime in Germany sought to eliminate schizophrenia from their "master race." In 1933, the Nazi government passed the Law for the Prevention of Progeny with Hereditary Diseases, under which approximately 400,000 Germans were sterilized without their consent for having conditions such as mental illness, epilepsy, "feeblemindedness"—a term that is now considered offensive, used to describe someone who was mentally challenged or not smart enough to take care of themselves—or physical deformities. Many more were killed in the gas chambers.

Following World War II and the atrocities of Nazi Germany, the United States saw a backlash to the eugenics movement, with many former supporters decrying it as a pseudoscience, or fake science with no evidence behind it. In 1974, the U.S. Department of Health, Education and Welfare (now known as the Department of Health and Human Services) issued official guidelines for sterilization procedures. The guidelines suspended the sterilization of women who were under the age of 21 or did not have the legal ability to provide consent. Furthermore, a 72-hour waiting period was mandated between the time when the consent form was signed and the actual procedure.

It was not until the 1950s, which saw the rise of antipsychotic medications, that individuals with schizophrenia began to receive true care. While not without certain side effects, these early medications did finally begin to reduce the symptoms of schizophrenia rather than simply sedating patients to make them easier for nurses to deal with.

Deinstitutionalization

The large increase in the number of patients housed in mental institutions between 1850 and 1950 strained the resources of these hospitals as funding was increasingly reduced. This combination of overcrowding and underfunding led to the return of the horrific treatments of the past.

Anthony Rudnicki was hospitalized at the Buffalo Psychiatric Center in 1961 following a mental breakdown related to bipolar disorder. Of his experience, he recalled, "My arms and legs were tied by twisted white sheets to the four corners of the bed. The light, I recall vividly, was nothing but a wire hanging from the ceiling with a naked bulb."[15] Unfortunately, Rudnicki's experience was not uncommon at the time.

Beginning in the 1960s, as conditions in these hospitals declined further, a growing concern for the civil rights of these patients began to rise. A shift toward community-centered mental health care emerged as new antipsychotic medications were discovered to help treat the symptoms of severe mental illnesses such as schizophrenia, and psychoanalysis was shown to provide further emotional support to patients outside of a hospital. This resulted in a mass exodus of mentally ill individuals out of state hospitals and the subsequent closure of many of those institutions. According to

PBS, 558,239 severely mentally ill patients were in the nation's public psychiatric hospitals in 1955. By 1994, there were only 71,619 patients. This meant around 92 percent of the people who would have been residents in one of these public psychiatric hospitals in 1955 were not residing there in 1994. Between 50 and 60 percent of these individuals were diagnosed with schizophrenia.

The motivating force behind deinstitutionalization was to give patients a less restrictive environment in which to recover, which worked well for individuals with less severe illnesses. In fact, with the proper support, many were able to live much richer lives outside of an institution. However, for the most vulnerable patients, many were left without the necessary support and care they required, leading to a rise in homelessness and incarceration (being sent to prison). According to PBS, between 1980 and 1995, the total number of prisoners in American prisons and jails increased 216 percent, from 501,886 to more than 1.5 million.

Despite this complicated and often devastating history, today's society is a much better place for individuals living with mental illness. Treatment options are far more humane, and new discoveries continue to be made as researchers dive deeper into the unknown aspects of the human brain and its functioning. Additionally, new legal protections and government services—including federal disability assistance, food stamps, and Medicaid programs—all play an essential role in helping individuals access the care and support they need to live their lives with dignity. However, more progress can still be made. Incarceration rates for the mentally ill continue to rise, demonstrating that society still has a long way to go in terms of understanding the best way to support and care for all its citizens.

CHAPTER TWO

THE DIAGNOSTIC PROCESS

Schizophrenia is a chronic mental disorder that can cause people to lose the ability to perceive and respond appropriately to their environment—a state known as psychosis—making it difficult for them to function at home, in school or work, and with friends. Schizophrenia affects more than 21 million people worldwide. In the United States, people with schizophrenia make up less than 1 percent of the population. Although it affects males and females about equally, symptoms typically begin to appear earlier in males (late teens and early 20s) than in females (late 20s and early 30s).

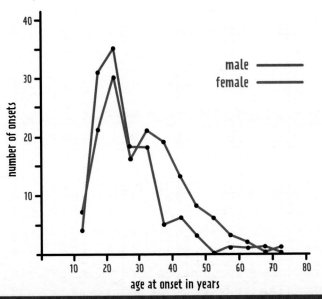

Males tend to show symptoms of schizophrenia earlier than females, as this information from Schizophrenia.com shows. This chart displays the results of one 1994 study that examined the age at which a certain number of people of each gender experienced the onset of schizophrenia symptoms.

Schizophrenia in Children

Childhood schizophrenia, though rare, can have a major impact on a child's development. The earliest symptoms—including delayed speech, unusual or late crawling, late walking, and abnormal behaviors such as arm flapping or rocking—are similar to those of certain developmental disorders, including autism, which makes diagnosis difficult.

The Mayo Clinic noted that some early signs of the disorder may be hard for parents to spot or may be easily attributed to the child's developmental stage. However, "symptoms may become more severe and more noticeable. Eventually, your child may develop the symptoms of psychosis, including hallucinations, delusions and difficulty organizing thoughts."[1] While it may be difficult to know what could be causing a change to a child's behavior, parents should consult with a pediatrician if their child:

- has stopped performing daily habits, such as bathing or dressing
- no longer wants to socialize
- starts slipping in academic performance
- shows a lack of emotion or displays emotions inappropriately
- displays violent or aggressive behavior

Other psychological disorders, such as depression and bipolar disorder, can cause similar symptoms, so a child psychiatrist may choose to monitor the child's behavior, perceptions, and thinking patterns for about six months before establishing a diagnosis. Early intervention for childhood schizophrenia is crucial, and treatment can help get symptoms under control before more serious complications develop. Additionally, establishing ongoing treatment as a routine can greatly improve a child's long-term outlook.

1. Mayo Clinic Staff, "Childhood Schizophrenia," Mayo Clinic, September 29, 2016. www.mayoclinic.org/diseases-conditions/childhood-schizophrenia/symptoms-causes/syc-20354483.

Risk Factors for Schizophrenia

In the past, people used to think that having cold or non-nurturing parents could cause schizophrenia. This idea of the "schizophrenogenic mother"—essentially, a mother who caused schizophrenia in her child—was established in 1948 by Frieda Fromm-Reichmann, a therapist and psychoanalyst who was expanding on an earlier theory of Sigmund Freud's.

According to Fromm-Reichmann, this type of parent was cold, bullying, and uninterested in their child's needs. They were overprotective and rejecting, resulting in their child's confusion and schizophrenic functioning. Blaming the parents provided an easy answer for why someone had schizophrenia, but research does not support this theory.

Today, researchers know there is no one single factor that leads to the disorder. For example, genetics play a role, but even if someone has a parent with schizophrenia, that does not mean the person definitely will develop the condition as well. Scientists believe a combination of genetics, individual brain chemistry, and certain environmental factors all determine whether a person will develop the disorder.

Some of the risk factors identified by researchers that can trigger schizophrenia include a family history of the disease; an overactive immune system; certain complications with pregnancy or birth, such as malnutrition, exposure to toxins, and viruses; and drug use during adolescence. One 2018 study found that problems such as preeclampsia (high blood pressure during pregnancy) that affect the placenta—an organ that protects and feeds the fetus while it is in the womb—contribute to a high risk of developing schizophrenia later in life.

Research suggests that marijuana use is a risk factor for schizophrenia. In fact, several meta-analyses (studies of many other studies' results) have found that marijuana use doubles the risk of developing psychotic symptoms or disorders later in life, even if the person takes no other drugs. Additionally, neuroimaging studies, or studies that look at brain structure, have revealed changes in both gray and white brain matter associated with heavy use of marijuana in both healthy subjects and patients who have already experienced at least one episode of psychosis.

While these findings imply that marijuana use plays a role in schizophrenia, it is not as straightforward as simple cause and effect. Not everyone who uses marijuana will develop schizophrenia; much like other risk factors, research suggests that additional factors play a role as well, including the age at which the individual began using marijuana and the amount of marijuana they typically use. One notable study found that those who started using marijuana when they were 15 years old or younger were at greater risk of developing symptoms of schizophrenia at 26 years of age than those who started when they were at least 18 years old.

Research has also shown that social factors such as living in a heavily urban area and experiencing childhood adversity or trauma—such as separation or loss of parents, abuse, stress, and social exclusion—may also play a role in the development of schizophrenia.

Race and Schizophrenia

Statistics show that members of immigrant groups, especially in Western Europe, and black people in the United States have much higher rates of schizophrenia than other groups. Some people believe this is due to genetics, but others believe it has to do with two factors: stress and racism.

Stress is not a mental illness, but it has been shown to make most mental illnesses worse. The stress of immigrating to a new place, especially if the person is escaping persecution in their former country or does not feel welcome in their new country, may make schizophrenia symptoms show up for the first time or become more apparent than they were previously.

Many black people in the United States also experience high amounts of stress, but the fact that black people—especially black men—are five times more likely than people of any other race to be

Black people, especially men, tend to be misdiagnosed with schizophrenia. Researchers believe this may be because a diagnosis of schizophrenia has historically been used as a way to dismiss black people's anger at racial injustice.

diagnosed with schizophrenia has prompted some professionals to take a closer look. Psychiatry professor Jonathan Metzl researched this issue after learning that Michigan's Ionia State Hospital, which treated those with mental illnesses and those determined to be "criminally insane," closed in 1972 and reopened not long after as a prison. What he learned disturbed him:

> By the mid- to late-1960s ... schizophrenia was a diagnosis disproportionately applied to the hospital's growing population of African American men from urban Detroit. Perhaps the most shocking evidence I uncovered was that hospital charts "diagnosed" these men in part because of their symptoms, but also because of their connections to the civil rights movement.[16]

Metzl explained that a change in the way schizophrenia was described in medical literature—"particularly terms such as 'hostility' and 'aggression'—was used to justify schizophrenia diagnoses in black men at Ionia in the 1960s and 1970s."[17] People who did not exhibit aggression, he said, were often rediagnosed with another disorder, even if their behavior had not changed. Other experts, including the National Alliance on Mental Illness (NAMI), agree that schizophrenia is likely overdiagnosed in black people, especially those who express anger or hostility over racial injustice. Black people who do have schizophrenia or another mental illness are also more likely to exhibit symptoms because they have more difficulty than other groups finding affordable, quality mental health care that helps them control their symptoms.

Another barrier to black people seeking help is the stigma that comes both from outside and inside their community. In an article for Shondaland.com—a website founded by Shonda Rhimes's company Shondaland, the TV production company that created shows such as *Grey's Anatomy* and *How to Get Away with Murder*—a black woman named GG Renee Hill wrote that while physical illnesses were discussed in detail in the black families she knew growing up, mental illnesses were kept secret. This came mainly from the feeling among the black community that they should not show any sort of weakness to avoid being further targeted by racism. In reality, as Hill learned when she got older, mental illness is not a weakness; this idea comes from misunderstandings about mental illnesses. However, it is an idea that is reinforced so often that many people, especially black people, feel they need to keep it a secret instead of getting the help they need.

Signs and Symptoms

It can be difficult for people to figure out if they are experiencing schizophrenia. In fact, many people with schizophrenia have no idea that is what is happening to them; they may refuse to acknowledge there is any issue at all. The inability of a person with a mental illness to realize that they are mentally ill is called anosognosia, and about 50 percent of people with schizophrenia experience it. Anosognosia causes people to believe that their hallucinations are real and that their behavior is rational, even if it is clear to those around them that neither of these things are true. Frequently, it is a parent, teacher, friend, or other close confidant who raises the flag that help is needed.

Schizophrenia can cause a range of problems, from disorganized thinking to disturbed emotions and unusual movement. The symptoms a person experiences can be mild or severe. Some symptoms may come and go over time, while others may always be present. Although symptoms can vary from person to person, they can be classified within one of three categories: positive symptoms, negative symptoms, and cognitive symptoms.

Positive symptoms may not sound like a problem because the word "positive" is often used to mean "good." However, in this context, the term actually describes excesses or additions to a person's behavior. The most common positive symptoms of schizophrenia are hallucinations, delusions, dysfunctional thinking, and catatonia, in which a person may move or talk in ways that are not normal for them or may become still and uncommunicative, all for seemingly no reason.

Flat affect, a symptom of schizophrenia, describes when people fail to show emotion on their face.

Negative symptoms are given this name because they describe losses or decreases in an individual's functioning. These symptoms can include reduced speaking, trouble starting and completing tasks, withdrawal from friends and family, and flat affect (lacking facial expressions or speaking in a monotone).

Cognitive symptoms can be mild or severe and include trouble focusing and paying attention, memory impairment, declining academic performance, and poor executive functioning (the ability to understand and use information to make decisions).

Hallucinations versus Delusions

Many people have difficulty understanding the difference between a hallucination and a delusion. Both describe things that are not real, but the difference is in the way the person perceives them. A hallucination is something a person actually sees, hears, or smells. It is not really there and is not apparent to anyone else, but the senses trick the person into believing it is real. The hallucination most commonly reported by people with schizophrenia is hearing voices.

In contrast, delusions are false beliefs that are in the mind only. There is no sensory proof of a delusion. For example, someone who has schizophrenia may believe they are incredibly rich even if there is no proof of this. They are not imagining piles of money in their living room; they simply believe wholeheartedly that there is a lot of money in their bank account. It is generally useless to try to convince someone that their hallucinations or delusions are not real because their mind develops new explanations for them as the old ones are disproved. For example, if someone who thought they were rich was shown a copy of their bank statement, they might insist that it was a fake statement or that their money had been stolen. One anonymous patient described their hallucinations and delusions: "I started to hear voices. The voices were degrading [insulting]. The radio started talking to me. I thought that people were conspiring against me. I was perplexed and disturbed."[1]

1. Anonymous, "Personal Stories: Recovering from Schizophrenia," NAMI, accessed on June 12, 2018. www.nami.org/Personal-Stories/Recovering-from-Schizophrenia.

"Negative symptoms … can be sometimes the first symptoms that people develop," said Dr. Melissa Heffler, a board-certified and licensed psychiatrist.

"They sort of withdraw, and families might say that they notice their child ... just kind of withdrawing more ... keeping in their room, not interacting with friends as much as they did, not interacting with family as much as they did ... not caring for themselves as properly as they had before, [including] limitations in hygiene."[18]

It is important to note that many of the signs and symptoms of schizophrenia are common in people with other issues, such as being under the influence of illegal drugs, experiencing side effects from a medication, or experiencing a period of depression. Some may not be attributed to a health problem at all; for example, many healthy people begin spending longer periods of time in their bedroom when they become teenagers. A doctor can help assess these symptoms and rule out alternative causes.

Symptoms typically start out mild and gradually progress in severity, ultimately leading to a psychotic episode in which the person may not be able to distinguish between what is real and what is not. Episodes of psychosis can be frightening for the patient because they cause delusions, distorted perceptions, and sometimes suicidal thoughts. Early intervention and treatment is extremely important to help get a patient's symptoms under control before they cause severe disruptions to that person's life.

At the Doctor's Office

Getting a diagnosis of schizophrenia generally involves ruling out anything else that could be causing the person's symptoms. First, a doctor conducts a physical exam and runs tests to rule out alcohol and drugs. Then, the person undergoes a psychiatric evaluation, in which they answer a number of questions about everything from their family medical history to their personal thoughts, feelings, actions, and any history of substance abuse. In addition to listening to the patient's answers and assessing the severity of their symptoms, the clinician also watches how the patient behaves and their overall appearance. This can help them determine the difference between someone who is wearing dirty clothes because they forgot to do laundry that week and someone who has stopped caring about their hygiene and appearance.

To diagnose schizophrenia, a doctor will conduct a physical exam and run tests to rule out other causes for the person's symptoms.

Parts of a Mental Status Exam

In addition to interviewing the patient about the symptoms they are experiencing, asking them about their family medical history, and observing their behavior, a doctor will also do a mental status exam to help establish a diagnosis. This exam assesses the person's mental functioning, including:

- **appearance:** Psychotic symptoms, such as disorganized thinking and behavior, can lead to an unusual appearance (such as odd clothing or hairstyle choices) as well as poor hygiene.

- **attitude:** Acting restless, anxious, suspicious of the doctor's motives, and unwilling to cooperate with the doctor can offer clues to the physician about what the patient may be experiencing.

- **behavior:** Mental health professionals also look for odd or unusual behaviors and movements, such as slowness, tics, unusual mannerisms, or odd posture.

- **speech:** Patients who are experiencing psychosis generally speak differently than normal (faster, slower, louder, softer, or in a monotone) and may not give appropriate answers to the questions they are asked.

- **mood:** Symptoms of depression or mania can help a doctor assess whether the issue is schizophrenia or a different disorder, such as bipolar disorder.

- **affect:** While "mood" is a person's own assessment of how they feel, "affect" describes what their body expresses about how they are feeling. This includes things such as facial expressions and tone of voice. Someone who says they feel happy but looks and sounds sad may be experiencing symptoms of schizophrenia.

- **thought process:** Psychosis can cause a disorganized thought process—how thoughts are put together. Patients with psychosis may show signs such as derailment (losing focus while speaking) or loosening of associations (jumping from one topic to another, unrelated one).

- **thought content:** The doctor will look for signs of delusional thoughts, paranoia, and hallucinations, as well as ask whether the patient is having suicidal thoughts or thoughts about harming others.

- **insight:** This refers to how well the patient understands their own illness, which can help the doctor gauge how well the person will stick to a treatment plan.

- **judgment:** This helps the doctor establish the patient's decision-making ability and estimates the likelihood of risky behaviors.

- **impulse control:** The doctor assesses how well the patient is able to stop themselves from engaging in dangerous or risky behavior. This also helps assess the patient's ability to think through decisions.

- **cognition:** The doctor also reviews the patient's cognitive functioning, including reasoning ability, memory, attention, and planning skills.

All of this information helps the mental health professional determine what forms of treatment would make the most sense for the patient to help reduce their symptoms and improve their quality of life.

A mental status exam helps a doctor assess their patient's mental functioning.

A doctor may also request certain lab tests to help establish a diagnosis. Blood and urine tests can check for drugs, infections, vitamin deficiencies, thyroid problems, liver or kidney diseases, and other issues. A neurologist may be asked to conduct an electroencephalogram (EEG), a test that measures the electrical activity in the brain. The EEG, which is painless, can help rule out seizure disorders such as temporal lobe epilepsy, which can cause psychosis-like symptoms, including hallucinations or delusions. Brain imaging tests, such as a computerized axial tomography (CAT) scan and magnetic resonance imaging (MRI), may also be conducted to help rule out brain tumors or infections. While these tests can rule out certain disorders, they cannot provide a definitive diagnosis of schizophrenia. In other words, they can only tell a doctor what the patient is not suffering from. Some doctors have also noted that flash electroretinography (fERG), a test eye doctors use to see how well the retinas of a person's eyes are working, could help diagnose schizophrenia. By using a portable fERG tool, researchers found that people with schizophrenia had some retinal abnormalities compared with people who did not have the disorder. However, more research must be done to make sure fERG gives accurate results before it can be routinely used as a diagnostic tool.

Once the mental health professional has combined all this information to form a picture of the patient's illness, they turn to the *Diagnostic and Statistical Manual of Mental Disorders (DSM)* to guide their diagnosis. Originally published in 1952 by the American Psychiatric Association (APA), the *DSM* is the authoritative guidebook used by health care providers to diagnose mental disorders. The APA explained, "It provides a common language for clinicians to communicate about their patients and establishes consistent and reliable diagnoses that can be used in the research of mental disorders."[19] The manual has been reviewed and revised four times since its original publication (The current edition is the *DSM-5*, published in 2013.) to address advances in research and understanding of mental disorders.

According to the *DSM-5*, in order to establish a diagnosis of schizophrenia, a person must display at least two symptoms—one of which must be delusions, hallucinations, or disorganized speech—and other disorders that might cause them must be ruled out. These symptoms must be present for at least six consecutive months; they can come and go, but they must be active for at least one month. The symptoms must be severe enough to interfere with a person's normal life and relationships with others.

Schizoaffective Disorder

Schizoaffective disorder is the term for a mental disorder that combines some symptoms of schizophrenia with some symptoms of a mood disorder such as bipolar disorder. It is not as well studied as other disorders, so doctors currently treat it the same way they would treat schizophrenia or bipolar disorder. Only about 0.3 percent of people develop schizoaffective disorder.

The symptoms of this disorder vary depending on the type of mood disorder the person experiences. For example, according to NAMI, "If a person has been diagnosed with schizoaffective disorder depressive type, they will experience feelings of sadness, emptiness, feelings of worthlessness or other symptoms of depression."[1] In contrast, if they are diagnosed with schizoaffective disorder bipolar type, they will experience symptoms of mania, such as risk-taking behavior and little need for sleep. Depressive type and bipolar type are the two major types of schizoaffective disorder. This mixture of symptoms makes it hard to diagnose; the main thing doctors look for is symptoms of a mood disorder that occur at the same time as symptoms of schizophrenia.

1. "Schizoaffective Disorder," NAMI, accessed on July 5, 2018. www.nami.org/Learn-More/Mental-Health-Conditions/Schizoaffective-Disorder.

According to Heffler, reaching a diagnosis of schizophrenia can be a long process, since symptoms can come and go, sometimes without the patient even realizing it. "Sometimes an individual can have an episode of psychosis that occurs once in their lifetime and it never recurs," she said. "So, it can be a long-term process."[20]

For some, receiving a diagnosis can be helpful; knowing what is going on in their body can be the first step in creating an action plan. However, for others, a diagnosis can feel like an unwanted label. It is important to remember that mental illness is just like physical illness, and it does not define someone as a person. As Heffler noted,

A comparison that I like to use is something like high blood pressure or diabetes; those are chronic medical issues that a lot of people accept and live with and they manage for the rest of their lives. I think it's important to lay out any mental illness in a similar way, because it is similar ... If you're dealing with a chronic illness ... you take medications, you stick with medications, and it helps manage the symptoms. For a lot of people, they take those medications and they can fulfill all their goals in their life ... We're not a diagnosis. We're an individual that's being treated for an illness.[21]

Likewise, with early intervention and proper treatment, individuals with schizophrenia can live independent and successful lives. Receiving the proper diagnosis is a critical first step in the recovery process, providing much-needed clarity and understanding.

CHAPTER THREE

THE BIOLOGY OF SCHIZOPHRENIA

As previously mentioned, there is no one single factor that causes a person to develop schizophrenia, the way a virus causes the common cold. Instead, schizophrenia results from a combination of risk factors, both internal (such as specific genes in the person's deoxyribonucleic acid, or DNA) and external (such as stressful life events or drug abuse). Since the 1960s, much research has been conducted to find out more about schizophrenia, what causes it, and what goes on inside the brain of a person with the disorder.

Although Emil Kraepelin was the first to determine a biological basis for schizophrenia in the late 1800s, it was not until many years later, as scientific research became more advanced, that people started to gain a more thorough understanding of what that really means.

All in the Family

Over the past few decades, researchers have discovered a hereditary component to schizophrenia, meaning something in a person's genes makes them more likely to develop the condition. Genes are the tiny instruction manuals that live inside a person's cells and determine what traits they have from each branch of the family tree—some from the mother's side and some from the father's. A groundbreaking study in Copenhagen, Denmark, analyzed adoption records of

Studies show a genetic link for schizophrenia, but having a family member with the disease does not necessarily mean a person will develop it.

more than 5,000 individuals to see which might have more of an impact on whether the adopted person developed schizophrenia: genetics or environment. Of the 5,500 adopted individuals, 33 had been diagnosed with schizophrenia, so the researchers looked at the mental health records of the biological and adoptive relatives of those 33 people, as well as those of 33 other adopted individuals who did not have the condition. Those without the condition were called the control group, and they were used for comparison. Researchers found that 14 percent of the biological relatives of the adoptees with schizophrenia were found to also have schizophrenia or a similar disorder, compared to only 2.7 percent of the adoptive relatives. In the control group, only 3.4 percent of biological relatives had the disorder, and 5.5 percent of adoptive relatives did as well. This clearly demonstrates a genetic link.

More recent studies have found similar results. Another study performed in Copenhagen, which was published in 2017, studied more than 30,000 pairs of twins and found that as much as 79 percent of the risk of developing schizophrenia may be due to genetics. The researchers came to their conclusion by comparing information from the Danish Twin Register, which is a public record of all the twins born in Denmark since 1870, and the Danish Psychiatric Central Research Register.

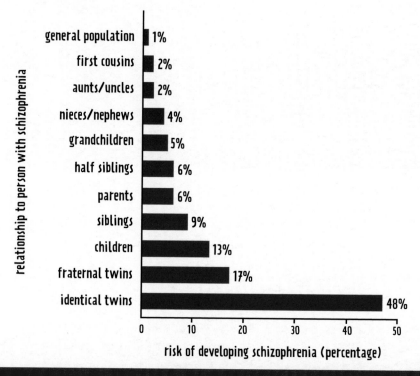

Schizophrenia has a genetic component, as this information from Schizophrenia.com shows. The fewer genes a person shares with a relative who has schizophrenia, the lower their risk of developing the disorder themselves. First cousins share only about 12.5 percent of their genes, while identical twins share about 100 percent.

Many people think of each specific gene as corresponding to a specific trait, but in reality, very few things are determined by one single gene. Even something as simple as eye color is determined by dozens of different genes. Similarly, schizophrenia is caused by a combination of gene defects. In analyzing DNA samples from large families and comparing gene fragments from members with and without the disorder, numerous studies have identified possible gene defects on 11 specific chromosomes, each of which may play a role in the development of schizophrenia.

In 2014, the Schizophrenia Working Group of the Psychiatric Genomics Consortium, which is a collaboration of more than 300 scientists from 35 countries, agreed with the underlying genetic basis of the disease. After comparing the DNA of about 37,000 people with schizophrenia with the DNA of more than 113,000 healthy subjects, the group claimed to have identified 128 gene variants connected with schizophrenia. These genes occupy 108 locations on the genome, with most of them having never been associated with the disorder previously.

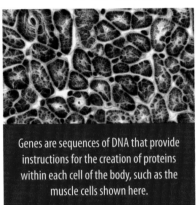

Genes are sequences of DNA that provide instructions for the creation of proteins within each cell of the body, such as the muscle cells shown here.

Understanding Genes

In the 1860s, botanist (a person who studies plants) Gregor Mendel published the first study to definitively prove that certain traits are passed on from one generation to the next. Mendel experimented with cross-breeding pea plants to see the effects on various physical characteristics, such as the height of the plant, the shape and color of the pods and seeds, and the color and position of the flowers. His work formed the basis of all future genetic research.

When people say something is inherited, it means a particular trait is passed from one generation to another through certain genes. Genes give the instructions that determine what traits a person will have, including what they look like and, to a certain extent, what they act like. Various combinations of genes determine everything from hair color to earlobe shape. They are what makes a person who they are, with the strands of DNA providing the specific instructions to make proteins (the building blocks of everything in the body). There are about 25,000 to 35,000 genes in every cell. They are found in the 46 chromosomes that live in the nucleus of each cell. Thanks to Mendel and his pea plants, today's scientists have a much better understanding of how traits are passed down through families, as well as how gene mutations can result in various illnesses.

Brain Chemistry and Schizophrenia

There are several different ways inherited genes could lead to schizophrenia. Genes provide the instructions to make proteins, which could be used to build larger structures—for example, organs such as the brain—or they could make smaller parts, such as neurotransmitters.

The most common theory regarding schizophrenia involves a neurotransmitter called dopamine. Neurons are specialized nerve cells within the brain that send messages to one another, controlling everything from behavior and perceptions to feelings and thoughts. These messages are sent by neurotransmitters, which are tiny chemicals that travel from one cell to another via synapses. The dopamine theory states that schizophrenia is caused by neurons firing too much dopamine, resulting in the symptoms of psychosis. This idea stems from the discovery of the first group of antipsychotic medications, called phenothiazines, in the 1950s. Researchers noticed that patients who underwent treatment with these drugs often developed muscle tremors similar to those experienced by people with Parkinson's disease. Parkinson's was already known to be caused by abnormally low levels of dopamine in particular areas of the brain. So, researchers reasoned, if the drugs reduced symptoms of psychosis while also causing these tremors, they were likely decreasing dopamine activity in the person's brain, suggesting that schizophrenia itself could be caused by too much dopamine.

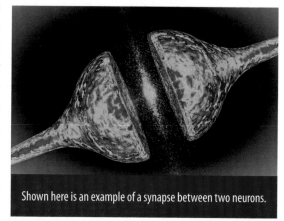

Shown here is an example of a synapse between two neurons.

Dopamine may not be the only neurotransmitter involved, however. Additional studies point toward a link between schizophrenia and other neurotransmitters. In 2014, researchers at Skaggs School of Pharmacy and Pharmaceutical Sciences at the University of California, San Diego, found that in patients with schizophrenia, the neurons secrete higher amounts of the neurotransmitters dopamine, epinephrine, and norepinephrine. These neurotransmitters have been thought to play a role in multiple psychiatric disorders, and several psychotropic drugs (drugs that treat psychosis) selectively target these neurotransmitters' activity in the brain. "The study provides new insights into neurotransmitter mechanisms in schizophrenia that can lead to new drug targets and therapeutics,"[22] said Vivian Hook, PhD, the senior author of the study.

Recently, researchers were able to determine that similar molecular changes in the brain occur in patients with schizophrenia and those with other neurological conditions, such as bipolar disorder and major depression. The study, published in *Science* in February 2018, looked at people's ribonucleic acid (RNA), a material that carries instructions from DNA to the proteins it controls. The researchers examined RNA in 700 samples from the brains of people with these neurological disorders and compared them with tissues from people who did not have any disorders.

As researchers gain a better understanding of changes in the brain and pinpoint the specific genes involved in the development of mental disorders, they hopefully will be able to develop more effective treatments and potentially cure these disorders. Additionally, this could help with diagnosis in the future. "It's possible that some of these changes might eventually show themselves in the blood or we might be able to develop new, noninvasive techniques for measuring gene expression in living patients down the road,"[23] said Dan Geschwind, head researcher of the RNA study and professor of neurology and psychiatry at the University of California, Los Angeles.

Learning from PCP

Phencyclidine (PCP) is a dissociative-anesthetic drug that some people take illegally for its mind-altering effects. Similar to ketamine—a veterinary tranquilizer that people sometimes illegally use as a recreational drug—PCP can cause hallucinations, delusions, cognitive problems, and a feeling of being detached from reality, all of which mimic symptoms of schizophrenia.

In the early 1980s, scientists discovered that PCP blocks the receptor for the neurotransmitter glutamate, which plays a crucial role in the brain's memory, learning, and perception functions. Too much glutamate can cause seizures and brain cell death, but too little can cause psychosis, coma, and death. About a decade later, scientists at Yale University found that activating certain glutamate receptors in rats could reverse the effects of PCP. This was the first proof that manipulating glutamate activity in the brain might help relieve the symptoms of psychosis. Following this discovery, numerous drug trials began to identify treatments that could reduce the symptoms of schizophrenia without producing the side effects of typical treatments, including severe weight gain and diabetes. An early clinical trial of a drug called LY2140023 by the pharmaceutical company Eli Lilly showed that the drug was slightly less effective than typical schizophrenia drug treatment, but it produced far fewer side effects while also improving cognition. Unfortunately, the drug failed in the third phase of testing in 2012, but researchers can use this information to find new ways to improve the lives of individuals with schizophrenia.

Brain Structure and Schizophrenia

In addition to abnormal brain chemistry, researchers have noted that the structure of the brain of individuals with schizophrenia also differs compared to people without the disorder. However, it is unclear whether these structural changes are a result of the disorder or the cause.

The brain goes through a lot of changes as a person grows from a baby to an adult, making all sorts of

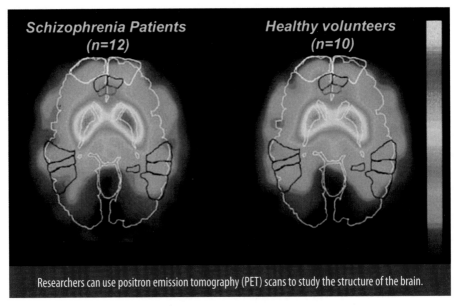

Schizophrenia Patients (n=12)

Healthy volunteers (n=10)

Researchers can use positron emission tomography (PET) scans to study the structure of the brain.

new connections and strengthening existing connections, thus allowing the person to learn. As they move from childhood toward adulthood, their brain starts to eliminate unnecessary connections in a process called synaptic pruning, which peaks in late adolescence. One popular theory regarding schizophrenia involves this pruning process. In 1983, University of California professor of psychiatry Irwin Feinberg hypothesized the disorder could be triggered by too much pruning of the cortical synapses on the surface of the brain, especially if it is accompanied by a failure to prune certain subcortical structures below the surface.

Previously, this theory was dismissed when other researchers found similar structural abnormalities in unaffected relatives of people with schizophrenia, which demonstrated that while each individual's genes may affect how the brain develops, those structural changes are not enough to cause the disorder on their own. However, in 2016, new findings made researchers reexamine the pruning theory. A team of scientists in Boston, Massachusetts, discovered a link between schizophrenia and an immune system protein called component 4 (C4), which plays a role in determining which neurons should be pruned. This could explain why the onset of schizophrenia generally occurs at the same time as a huge loss of synapses. The researchers compared the DNA of people with schizophrenia to the DNA of people without it. At first, it seemed as though there was no specific DNA variation associated with the disease, but eventually they found a pattern: "Many of the DNA variations seemed to affect the amount of a specific type of C4 protein present in the synapses of the brain. And the more C4 was present, the higher the risk of developing schizophrenia."[24] Because there are multiple types of C4, this pattern was hard to see initially. Based on this research, the current theory is that too much of this specific type of C4 causes too many neurons to be pruned, which leads to the brain changes—such as thinning tissue—that are often seen in schizophrenia patients.

In 2011, psychiatric researchers Gabor Faludi and Karoly Mirnics published a review that cited 60 references to Feinberg's theory "and endorsed the growing consensus that schizophrenia is 'a mental disorder with a complex etiology [cause] that arises as an interaction between genetic and environmental factors.'"[25]

In April 2013, President Barack Obama announced his Brain Research through Advancing Innovative Neurotechnologies (BRAIN) Initiative, which aims to develop and apply new technologies to create a more complete understanding of the brain in action, providing important information for researchers who are looking for new ways to treat, cure, and possibly prevent brain disorders. The results of the first BRAIN-funded study, published in 2015, demonstrated that an animal's behavior could be changed by manipulating its brain circuitry, specifically identifying the neurons involved in a particular behavior and activating or deactivating them accordingly. In the study, researchers targeted hunger-promoting neurons, making the mice either ignore food bowls or eat enthusiastically. When they targeted movement neurons instead, the mice scampered or stopped. This could lead to breakthrough treatments for psychiatric disorders, allowing doctors to tailor therapies to the patient's underlying miswiring. "This tool sharpens the cutting edge of research aimed at improving our understanding of brain circuit disorders, such as schizophrenia and addictive behaviors,"[26] said Dr. Francis Collins, director of the National Institutes of Health (NIH).

All of this research makes it clear that identifying one single factor that leads to schizophrenia is just not possible. The brain is a complex organ, and scientists are still trying to understand how all the complicated circuitry and chemistry works together to make humans function—or fail to function. Genes obviously play a role, impacting the way the brain develops and which chemicals are present in certain amounts, but genetics do not tell the whole story. Environmental triggers, such as exposure to certain viruses prenatally (before birth), poor nutrition during pregnancy, and early drug use can increase the chances of developing schizophrenia, particularly in individuals who are already genetically predisposed to the condition.

CHAPTER FOUR

TREATING SCHIZOPHRENIA

Although there is no cure for schizophrenia currently, there are several treatments available to help reduce the symptoms and manage the disorder. Early psychosis can be terrifying, both for the individual experiencing symptoms and for friends and family who do not understand what is happening to their loved one. However, the earlier a person can begin treatment, the better their chances are of recovery.

A 2008 study conducted by the National Institute of Mental Health (NIMH) showed that coordinated specialty care (CSC) programs are significantly better at helping people with early psychosis improve than care that is typically provided in community settings. CSC treatment programs help patients and families connect with providers for care and support as they embark on the road to recovery. CSC programs involve a team of care specialists who create an individualized treatment plan for patients. Depending on the person's needs, their treatment plan may include a primary therapist, medication treatment, a family education program, peer support groups, a supported education and employment specialist to assist in setting and reaching goals, and case management services to assist with any additional needs the patient might have, such as transportation, housing, or legal assistance.

Depending on the severity of the patient's symptoms and whether they pose a danger to themselves or others, a mental health professional may recommend hospitalization, which can be voluntary or involuntary. Voluntary inpatient treatment means the patient willingly signs in to the hospital. Involuntary hospitalization, also referred to as civil commitment or compulsory treatment, is when a doctor determines the patient's symptoms are severe enough to require inpatient treatment but the patient does not consent. Involuntary treatment depends on local, state, and national laws, and it can last from several days to a couple of weeks or longer. Once the patient's psychosis begins to subside, they can switch from inpatient to outpatient treatment. Outpatient commitment is typically court ordered to ensure the patient stays in treatment. If they fail to continue the outpatient treatment, the patient may be hospitalized again. However, it can be difficult for someone to be admitted to a hospital unless their symptoms are extremely severe and they present an immediate, clear threat to themselves or others. This is due to a lack of funding and a lack of space in hospitals. Sadly, officials must often choose only the patients who are experiencing the worst symptoms to be admitted, which means many people who could benefit from inpatient care go untreated.

Voluntary treatment is obviously ideal, as it helps strengthen the relationship between the patient and their care team, as well as improve treatment outcomes. Hospitalization is often feared due to the unethical practices of past mental institutions, but today, people who work with patients who are mentally ill generally have better training and more humane guidelines. Unfortunately, though, abuse does sometimes still happen, and the most vulnerable patients may not be able to do anything about it. This is why it is important for hospitals and prisons to have outside observers, such as government officials, overseeing the conditions in which patients with mental illnesses are kept.

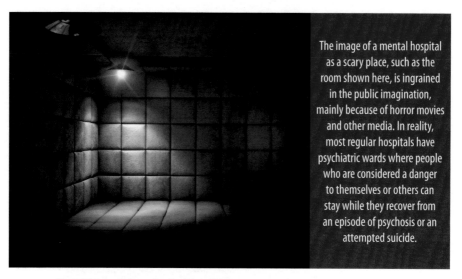

The image of a mental hospital as a scary place, such as the room shown here, is ingrained in the public imagination, mainly because of horror movies and other media. In reality, most regular hospitals have psychiatric wards where people who are considered a danger to themselves or others can stay while they recover from an episode of psychosis or an attempted suicide.

Getting Mental Health Treatment without Insurance

There may be a number of reasons why a person does not seek treatment for their mental illness, including anosognosia and fear of the stigma of being in therapy. One of the most common reasons is lack of health insurance or having health insurance that does not cover therapy, which can be expensive, especially if someone needs multiple sessions per week. Fortunately, there are some ways this problem can be solved. Licensed Specialist Clinical Social Worker (LSCSW) Danielle Miller offered ways people can access therapy even if they are uninsured:

- **in-school services:** High school students "who have been diagnosed through the public school system by an appointed school psychologist and have a qualified Individualized Education Plan (IEP) may be eligible for free therapeutic services."[27] College students can reach out to their school's counseling center or health center for information about free or reduced-cost treatment.

- **sliding-fee scale:** Many care providers offer treatment on a sliding scale, meaning the fee is based on the patient's income and the people that income supports. Sessions typically last about 1 hour, and services may be available for as low as $10 per session if someone meets the financial criteria. Local providers can answer questions about their sliding scale options.

- **free services:** It can be difficult for people to find free resources, but they do exist. Churches and other community organizations are a good place to start. However, some people misrepresent themselves as therapists to take advantage of people who are looking for help. Miller advised, "If you aren't sure whether an organization is legitimate, ask about their licensure. Simply ask: 'Do you hold a clinical license?' Any therapist who is qualified will be credentialed, according to their state laws. You aren't just being nosy. You have a right to this information."[28]

Additionally, all state Medicaid programs—government-provided health insurance for people who live in poverty—offer some mental health services. The Children's Health Insurance Program (CHIP) also provides a full array of services to beneficiaries. These services can include counseling, help managing medication, social work services, and substance use disorder treatment. Someone who is suicidal and in need of immediate help can contact the National Suicide Prevention Lifeline for free at any time. The crisis workers there can provide counseling and mental health referrals.

Medications for Schizophrenia

Medication is generally a key component of treating the symptoms of schizophrenia. However, antipsychotic medications tend to produce various side effects in addition to curbing symptoms, so finding the right balance of medication types and dosages to maximize the benefits with the least amount of side effects can be a challenge. When creating a care plan for a patient, Heffler explained that it is important to first take into consideration the individual's symptoms and any other health issues that could be affected by a particular medication and its side effects. There are more than 60 antipsychotic medications used around the world, about 20 of which are available in the United States, giving psychiatrists many options to tailor treatment for their patients.

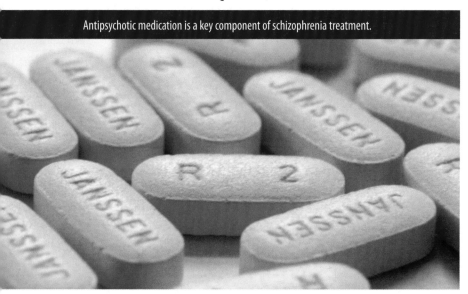

Antipsychotic medication is a key component of schizophrenia treatment.

First-generation antipsychotic medications (FGAs) were developed in the 1950s and include drugs such as chlorpromazine or haloperidol. Also known as typical, conventional, or classic antipsychotics; neuroleptics; and dopamine antagonists, FGAs work by reducing dopamine neurotransmission. They do this by blocking certain receptors in the four dopamine pathways in the brain. These medicines work well at reducing positive symptoms, such as hallucinations, delusions, and paranoia. However, they are not as effective at treating negative symptoms or cognitive dysfunction.

They can also cause various movement disorders, with symptoms that include restlessness; repetitive, involuntary muscle movements; or an inability to move. They also include less serious side effects such as dry mouth, blurry vision, constipation, headache, and drowsiness. Though rare, the drugs also may cause neuroleptic malignant syndrome—a potentially life-threatening condition that causes fever and muscle stiffness—and tardive dyskinesia, an adverse event that develops over an extended period of time and causes abnormal, involuntary movements. Although every medicine comes with the risk of side effects, not every patient will experience them. If the patient does experience any side effects, the prescribing doctor may recommend waiting it out if it is a side effect that tends to disappear after a few days or weeks. If it does not go away on its own or is a more serious side effect, the doctor may decrease the dose, change the way the patient takes the medicine, add another medicine to counter the side effect, or switch to a different medicine that will hopefully not cause the side effect.

Second-generation antipsychotic medications (SGAs), also called atypical antipsychotics, were developed in the 1990s. These newer medications bind to certain receptors for the neurotransmitter serotonin, in addition to dopamine receptors. Atypical antipsychotics are effective at reducing positive symptoms of psychosis and are more effective at treating negative symptoms and cognitive dysfunction, compared to older medicines. Importantly, SGAs are less likely to cause movement disorders or tardive dyskinesia. There are more than 10 atypical antipsychotic medications in use around the world. Although they are considered the first-choice medicines for treating psychosis, they are generally more expensive than the conventional antipsychotics. While some of the potential side effects of SGAs are similar to conventional antipsychotics—including blurry vision, constipation, dizziness, dry mouth, sleepiness, and low blood pressure—these medications can also cause weight gain and metabolic side effects. Patients taking this class of medicine may need to undergo periodic check-ups, including blood tests and weigh-ins, so the doctor can watch out for these side effects. Clozapine, an atypical antipsychotic that is most helpful for treatment-resistant psychosis, can cause a number of serious adverse effects, including myocarditis (inflammation of the heart muscles), seizures, and agranulocytosis (a sudden decrease in white blood cells that leaves the patient at risk for severe infections). Due to these risks, clozapine is typically used only after other medications have failed, and patients must have weekly or biweekly blood tests to closely monitor their white blood cell counts.

A doctor can help a patient evaluate the benefits and risks of conventional antipsychotic medication versus atypical medicines. FGAs are more likely to cause neurological problems, while SGAs tend to cause weight gain and other issues with a person's metabolism.

To decide which medication is right for each patient, doctors must weigh a number of factors to tailor the treatment to their patient's individual needs. According to *The First Episode of Psychosis: A Guide for Patients and Their Families*, these factors include:

- *whether or not the medicine helped in the past*
- *the specific symptoms present*
- *past side effects or expected side effects*
- *how easy it is to take the medicine (for example, once rather than twice daily)*
- *the cost of the medicine*
- *the doctor's own familiarity with specific medicines*
- *whether or not a family member ever benefited from the medicine*[29]

"You have a class of medications that you typically start with," Heffler explained, "and then you look at the individual and their specific needs, what they bring to the table, and tailor what medication you think might be appropriate for them at that time."[30] Sometimes a drug's side effects can even be helpful. For instance, if a patient is experiencing anxiety or difficulty sleeping, then a medicine with a side effect of sleepiness might be beneficial for that person.

Consistently taking medications is crucial for patients with schizophrenia. Approximately 85 percent of patients with first-episode psychosis stop having symptoms after about three months of taking an antipsychotic medication. In addition to reducing symptoms and aiding recovery, antipsychotic medications help reduce the risk of relapse and hospitalization. For patients who may have difficulty taking their medication consistently, there are several antipsychotic medications available as a shot that is given every two to four weeks.

Researchers continue to work to discover new medications that can effectively treat schizophrenia with the fewest negative side effects possible. As most available treatments mostly affect the positive symptoms of psychosis, a lot of current studies are focused on developing medicines that will also treat negative symptoms and cognitive dysfunction, which can be particularly debilitating for patients. Several studies from 2013 to 2018 have suggested that natural supplements—particularly B vitamins such as folic acid and B12—can help with negative symptoms when combined with antipsychotic medications. Additionally, an antipsychotic called MIN-101 reduced negative symptoms in clinical trials. However, as of 2018, it is still in the experimental stage.

Conventional versus Atypical Antipsychotics

All medications can cause side effects, though not every person taking a medication will experience them. It is important for patients to discuss the potential side effects of any medication with their doctor so they know what to look for and so their doctor can help manage those effects. FGAs are associated with an increased risk of certain neurological side effects, such as tardive dyskinesia, whereas SGAs are associated with increased risk of metabolic side effects, including high blood sugar and weight gain. While none of those side effects are ideal, the medications work well to reduce psychotic symptoms, which is important. Researchers have evaluated whether one class of medications is more effective than the other. According to the Psychopharmacology Institute, there are two important sets of clinical trials that shed some light on this question. The first are the Clinical Antipsychotic Trials of Intervention Effectiveness, funded by NIMH. The other is the Cost Utility of the Latest Antipsychotics in Severe Schizophrenia, funded by the United Kingdom's National Health Service.

According to the results from these trials:

- There is no evidence that SGAs are better than FGAs in the treatment of schizophrenia's negative symptoms.

- Clozapine (the first SGA drug to be approved) has shown clear improvement in schizophrenia that is reistant to other forms of treatment.

Psychosocial Interventions

Unlike many physical illnesses, for which taking a daily medication may be all that is required to help a patient recover, mental illness treatment generally requires a more holistic approach. This means treating all aspects of a disorder in a way that is connected. As Dr. Heffler noted, "A medication can treat symptoms, but we're human beings. We're more complicated than that, we're not just symptoms ... we have personality, we have different traits and character that we bring to the table."[31] Once a patient's symptoms start to become manageable with medication, their treatment team can begin to look at other aspects of the disorder that are affecting the patient's well-being. Because schizophrenia often develops in late adolescence and early adulthood, when people's psychological and social skills mature, many people with the disorder experience psychosocial problems, including difficulties at school, at work, in relationships, or in other social environments. "When we look at a holistic approach to treatment of really anything, it has to involve not just the psychiatric side of things, but also the psychological and emotional side of things—that individual and what they enjoy in life and finding fulfillment in that,"[32] Heffler said.

The goal of psychosocial treatment is to help patients overcome these problems and improve their psychosocial skills to the best possible level of functioning so they can live their best lives.

According to the Mayo Clinic, forms of psychosocial interventions can include:

- *Individual therapy. Psychotherapy may help to normalize thought patterns. Also, learning to cope with stress and identify early warning signs of relapse can help people with schizophrenia manage their illness.*

- *Social skills training.* This focuses on improving communication and social interactions and improving the ability to participate in daily activities.
- *Family therapy.* This provides support and education to families dealing with schizophrenia.
- *Vocational rehabilitation and supported employment.* This focuses on helping people with schizophrenia prepare for, find and keep jobs.[33]

The most common form of therapy for patients with schizophrenia is cognitive behavioral therapy (CBT), which focuses on practical solutions to problems. CBT clinicians encourage patients to challenge their odd and disordered thoughts and help them change their behavior.

Another form of individual therapy is cognitive enhancement therapy (CET), which works to promote cognitive functioning and boost a person's confidence in their thinking skills. CET involves using both group sessions and computer-based brain training. According to NAMI, as of 2018, researchers are actively working to find out more about this therapy.

In addition to individual therapy, which helps patients address their symptoms on a one-on-one basis, group therapy can be used to help patients feel less alone, allowing them to connect with others who are going through similar problems. The three most common forms of this type of therapy are psychoeducational groups, therapy groups, and activity groups. Psychoeducational groups teach patients about their illness, including its symptoms, its treatment, its warning signs, and other aspects of psychosis. Therapy groups let patients focus on their relationships with others, their coping skills, and identifying the stressors that make their symptoms worse. Activity groups work on developing social skills, confidence, and sometimes job skills.

Group therapy helps patients feel less alone as they interact with other people who are dealing with similar issues.

There are several forms of family interventions as well, which help families of people with mental illness cope with stress, improve their social supports, and learn to combat the effects of stigma. Having a stable support system is incredibly valuable for a patient's recovery, so supporting family members helps everyone. Family interventions include family psychoeducation—which teaches families about the illness their loved one has and what they can expect over time—and family therapy, which focuses on stressors in the patient's environment and can be useful in preventing a relapse of psychosis.

Additional Care Concerns

People with severe mental illnesses such as schizophrenia are at a statistically higher risk of developing physical ailments such as diabetes, heart problems, and lung disease, partially due to the disorder's effect on their executive functioning skills—they are less

Loved ones can play an important role in helping a person with schizophrenia stick to their treatment plan.

likely to take care of their bodies. They are also more likely to struggle with substance abuse issues, which can impact not only the effectiveness of their treatment but also how well the person sticks to their treatment plan. As such, individuals with schizophrenia and their loved ones must take extra care to ensure the person's physical well-being is as closely monitored as their mental and emotional well-being.

NAMI offers the following suggestions for individuals with schizophrenia on managing their own physical and emotional well-being to help prevent a coexisting illness, which is called a comorbidity:

- *Manage Stress. Stress can trigger psychosis and make the symptoms of schizophrenia worse, so keeping it under control is extremely important. Know your limits, both at home and at work or school. Don't take on more than you can handle and take time to yourself if you're feeling overwhelmed.*

- *Try to get plenty of sleep. When you're on medication, you most likely need even more sleep than the standard eight hours. Many people with schizophrenia have trouble with sleep, but lifestyle changes such as getting regular exercise and avoiding caffeine can help.*

- *Avoid alcohol and drugs. It's indisputable that substance abuse affects the benefits of medication and worsens symptoms. If you have a substance abuse problem, seek help.*

- *Maintain connections. Having friends and family involved in your treatment plan can go a long way towards recovery. People living with schizophrenia often have a difficult time in social situations, so surrounding yourself with people who understand this can make the transition back into daily social life smoother. If you feel you can, consider joining a schizophrenia support group or getting involved with a local church, club, or other organization.*[34]

For friends and family members of individuals with schizophrenia, NAMI offers the following suggestions for supporting a loved one coping with psychosis:

- *Respond calmly. To your loved one, the hallucinations seem real, so it doesn't help to say they are imaginary. Calmly explain that you see things differently. [Be] respectful without tolerating dangerous or inappropriate behavior.*

- *Pay attention to triggers. You can help your family member or friend understand, and try to avoid, the situations that trigger his or her symptoms or cause a relapse or disrupt normal activities.*

- *Help ensure medications are taken as prescribed. Many people question whether they still need the medication when they're feeling better, or if they don't like the side effects. Encourage your loved one to take his or her medication regularly to prevent symptoms from coming back or getting worse.*

- *Understanding lack of awareness (anosognosia).* Your family member or friend … may be unable to see that he or she has schizophrenia. Rather than trying to convince the person he or she has schizophrenia, you can show support by helping him or her be safe, get therapy, and take the prescribed medications.

- *Help avoid drugs or alcohol.* These substances are known to worsen schizophrenia symptoms and trigger psychosis. If your loved one develops a substance use disorder, getting help is essential.[35]

Finding the right combination of therapy and medication can be a long and sometimes frustrating process, but doctors as well as patients say it is worth it. If the patient shows improvement over time, they may be able to reduce their medication dosage, which can also reduce the impact of any side effects they experience. Andrew Wiese, a patient with schizophrenia, explained,

> During the last 15 months I have been receiving care … I believe I have gotten much better. My psychotic symptoms such as paranoia and delusions have gone away. I have grown closer to my family with the help of therapy and an excellent therapist. My existing friendships have also been strengthened, and I have made new friends through my support groups. My antipsychotic dosage has been lowered and may be reduced again in the future.[36]

Some people are eventually able to stop taking medication altogether. One 2017 study found that after 10 years of treatment, 30 percent of patients are able to stop taking antipsychotics without seeing a return of their symptoms. According to the study, women who do not take other kinds of drugs have the highest level of functionality after stopping their medication. However, the researchers noted that "the study is probably not representative of all patients who suffer from schizophrenia."[37] Each person's body and brain chemistry are different, and no one should stop taking their medication without consulting their doctor first. Many people with schizophrenia need to be on medication for life, which means they must learn how to live the best life they can in spite of their illness.

CHAPTER FIVE

LIVING WITH MENTAL ILLNESS

Once a person receives a diagnosis, they can begin the journey toward recovery. Although schizophrenia is an incurable, chronic disorder, it is not a death sentence. In fact, research shows that with proper treatment, many can experience significant recovery and live relatively normal lives, with their own residence, a job, and friends and family. In one study, which was published in 2005, psychologist Martin Harrow of the University of Illinois College of Medicine led a team of researchers that followed patients over a period of 15 years. The researchers found that about 40 percent of the patients experienced periods of significant recovery. They defined this in terms of the absence of severe symptoms as well as the ability to work, enjoy social activities, and live outside a hospital for one year or more.

Why Is a Diagnosis Important?

Some individuals may fear a diagnosis; they may be hesitant to accept it or worry about the stigma that often is attached to mental illness. However, a diagnosis can be life-changing. With a solid diagnosis comes understanding—an explanation for why a person has been feeling and experiencing certain things that seem so surreal. Diagnosis also leads to treatment tailored specifically to the individual's needs and care providers who understand and can provide support and guidance. Although fostering and

Famous People with Schizophrenia

Schizophrenia affects more than 21 million people worldwide. Although symptoms can be severe and disabling, many individuals with the disease are able to live full lives and achieve great things with treatment. Here are a few examples of famous individuals who had schizophrenia:

- **John Nash Jr.:** Nash was an American mathematician who was awarded the Nobel Prize for Economics in 1994 for his work on the mathematics of game theory. The Academy Award-winning film *A Beautiful Mind*, based on a book of the same name, was about Nash's life. Though the film differs in a number of ways from Nash's real life, it does offer audiences a glimpse into the slow progression of psychosis as well as some of the side effects of antipsychotic medications that often lead patients to stop treatment (as Nash chose to do both in the film and real life).

John Nash's episodes of psychosis caused him to believe he could understand messages from aliens and that he was going to be the emperor of Antarctica. In spite of this, he created mathematical theories that are still used today in economics and other areas.

- **Lionel Aldridge:** Aldridge was an American professional football player who played defensive end in the National Football League (NFL) for 11 seasons with the Green Bay Packers and San Diego Chargers, winning 2 Super Bowls with the Packers. He later became an advocate for the homeless and mentally ill.

- **Syd Barrett:** Barrett was an English singer, songwriter, and musician, best known as a founding member of the band Pink Floyd.

maintaining relationships with others may be difficult for people with schizophrenia, the benefit of having an understanding, listening ear is immeasurable for anyone dealing with mental illness.

In addition, receiving a diagnosis can help in a number of practical ways. It informs health insurance companies that the individual has a condition that requires medical care, making it easier to access that care. A diagnosis is also necessary to qualify for federal programs such as disability support and job protection. The Americans with Disabilities Act (ADA) forbids discrimination against job applicants and employees with disabilities, and the Family Medical Leave Act (FMLA) allows up to 12 weeks of unpaid leave for employees in the event of an illness while preserving their job placement and benefits. Some people living with schizophrenia may find that there are periods of time when working becomes too difficult and they can no longer maintain employment. During those times, they may be eligible for Social Security Disability Insurance (SSDI) benefits and Supplemental Security Income (SSI) to help them afford the things they need while they are in between jobs.

Schizophrenia and Homelessness

Because schizophrenia typically arises during the time when people develop critical social and self-sufficiency skills, it can be difficult for individuals with the disorder to integrate into society without assistance. Unfortunately, some individuals with schizophrenia become homeless. According to NAMI, approximately 26 percent of adults staying in homeless shelters have a serious mental illness. Additionally, about 70 percent of young adults in the juvenile justice system have at least one mental illness, and at least 20 percent have a serious mental illness such as schizophrenia. On average, adults in the United States who have a serious mental illness die 25 years earlier than others, mainly due to treatable medical conditions. Lack of treatment frequently leads to suicide.

Schizophrenia can make it difficult for people to maintain employment, which can lead to homelessness.

Having a safe place to live is a basic necessity for any person. For someone with schizophrenia, it can provide the stability they need to recover from their illness and help prevent hospitalization and incarceration. Housing options can range from completely independent to round-the-clock care, depending on the person's needs and financial ability. Supportive housing, partially supervised group housing, and supervised group housing are all options for those who require varying levels of assistance. Those who are more independent and able to take care of their basic needs and manage their medication can look at rental housing or home ownership. The U.S. Department of Housing and Urban Development (HUD) offers several housing assistance and counseling programs, including the Housing Choice Voucher Program (Section 8), which helps low-income families, the elderly, and the disabled gain public housing, and the Supportive Housing for People with Disabilities Program (Section 811), which provides housing for people who have disabilities and requires that all housing has access to supportive services such as case management and employment assistance.

Preventing a Relapse

Recovery is a long-term process, and many people with schizophrenia will experience a relapse, or recurrence, of their psychotic symptoms at some point. Staying in treatment and consistently taking any pre-scribed medication can help prevent relapse. However, it is important to understand and be able to detect the early warning signs and know what to do if they begin to develop. These warning signs will vary from person to person, just as the disorder itself varies from person to person, though there are some common warning signs to be aware of, including:

- changes in mood, such as sadness, nervousness, or irritability

- sleep disturbances, such as insomnia (inability to fall or stay asleep), hypersomnia (sleeping more than usual), or sleeping during the day and being awake all night

- ideas of reference, which means the individual thinks that others are talking to or about them when they are not (for example, believing someone on TV is speaking about them)

- feelings of suspicion toward others

- unusual ideas, such as magical thinking (believing their thoughts can influence events or other people's behav-iors) or being confused about what is real or imaginary

- trouble concentrating

- brief, intermittent hallucinations

- deterioration in role functioning, which means the individual is becoming less able to perform daily activities

- social withdrawal

- avolition, which means a lack of motivation or ability to start and complete tasks

- decreased emotional expression

The better a person and their family can identify early warning signs, the sooner they can take action to avoid hospitalization. If warning signs begin to develop, it is important for the person and their supporters to discuss them openly to help determine whether these signs could have other explanations not related to their illness. The person's doctor should also be contacted to discuss whether an adjustment in medication is needed or if any other changes in treatment could be helpful. Since warning signs often appear as a result of the person stopping their medication, it is important to check their medication plan and consider watching them more closely to make sure they are sticking to the treatment plan. Efforts should also be made to reduce or stop any substance abuse. Sometimes reducing a person's stress level—either by cutting back on responsibilities, looking for new opportunities for relaxing activities, or resolving a stressful conflict—can help avoid a relapse as well. A counselor or support group may be a good way to help the person learn and use coping techniques.

What Not to Say

It takes courage for someone with schizophrenia to tell others about their condition. The way the disease is shown in the media gives many people incorrect ideas about it, which sometimes makes them say things that are offensive. Below are some things people should never say to someone with schizophrenia.

- "Are you off your meds?"
- "You're just being delusional."
- "But you don't look sick."
- "What do the voices tell you?"
- "Just don't listen to the voices."
- "You know [hallucination/delusion] isn't real, right?"
- "How many personalities do you have?"
- "Are you dangerous?"
- "You should try [diet/exercise/yoga/alternative treatment]."

A Return to the Bad Old Days

In 1963, the U.S. Congress passed the Community Mental Health Act, which created the requirements for the community-based care of the mentally ill that are in effect today, including outpatient therapy, inpatient treatment, emergency care, preventive care, and aftercare. This law jump-started the decades-long process of deinstitutionalization, in which hundreds of thousands of patients moved from state institutions to local communities. While community-based care can be very effective for treating schizophrenia, this assumes that an individual can access those services. Unfortunately, community care centers are facing some of the same issues that state institutions of the past ran into, including more patients than can be supported with the scarce funding and resources available. As a result of deinstitutionalization, hundreds of thousands of individuals have become caught in a cycle of homelessness, hospitalization, and incarceration. Nearly 400,000 of the 2.2 million prisoners in the United States have a psychiatric diagnosis. In fact, according to a 2018 article in *Esquire* magazine, 10 out of every 11 psychiatric patients housed by the government are behind bars.

Approximately 21 percent of local prisoners and 20 percent of state prisoners have a history of mental illness.

It is easy to see how this could happen: When encountering a person experiencing a psychotic episode, people may be more likely to call the police than to rush the individual to the emergency room. In an interview with PBS *NewsHour*, Alex Briscoe, the health director for Alameda County in northern California, explained, "We've, frankly, criminalized the mentally ill, and used local jails as de facto mental health institutions."[38] Other experts say similar things. Paul Gionfriddo, the president and CEO of Mental Health America, said in an interview, "As a person who was a state elected official in Connecticut 40 years ago, I toured state psychiatric facilities at that time, and I can tell you that they not only look identical to our prisons today, but the prisons are often in the same exact buildings that were once the state mental hospitals."[39]

Prisons do provide psychiatric care for inmates. Every person who is incarcerated undergoes a mental health assessment when they first arrive to determine the amount of care they may need and decide which institution is equipped to house them. Inmates are provided any medications they may need, and counselors are available as well. However, prison is not a good place for someone to recover. The stress of incarceration and the social environment in prisons can make mental illness worse. Additionally, it is much more expensive to treat prisoners with mental health conditions than it would be to fund community-based care. Prisons also do not have the same ethical standards of care as mental health facilities, which leads to violations of the patients' rights. For example, mentally ill patients in hospitals are almost never tied down or put in straitjackets because experts have learned how to talk to a distressed patient in a way that calms them down. In contrast, prison guards are more likely to restrain an inmate than talk to them, and they have been frequently found to use restraints as punishment.

In 2010, the American Bar Association issued guidelines saying that prisons should not use physical restraints such as handcuffs or straitjackets to punish any prisoner for less-than-ideal behavior, such as yelling, insulting guards, or other unpleasant but nonviolent behavior. The guidelines state that restraints should only be used in cases where the prisoner poses an immediate threat to themselves, others, or prison property, or when they are being transported from one building to another (such as from the courthouse to the prison). The restraints should be removed as soon as any danger has passed.

Difficulty Adjusting In and Out of Prison

The *Esquire* article also gave an example of one of the ways inmates with mental illness have difficulty adjusting to prison life:

> [Joe's] daily slew of medications exhausted him, making it a challenge to follow the simplest procedures. To go to the mess hall for meals or the yard for recreation, you had to be "on your bars"—standing by your cell door—at a certain time each

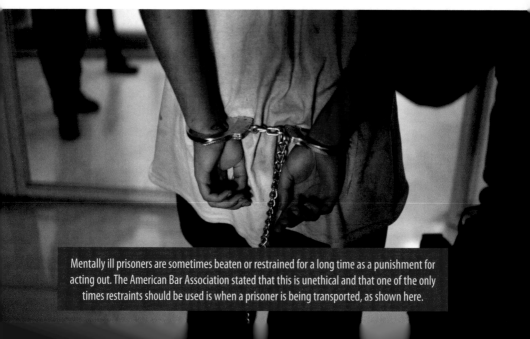

Mentally ill prisoners are sometimes beaten or restrained for a long time as a punishment for acting out. The American Bar Association stated that this is unethical and that one of the only times restraints should be used is when a prisoner is being transported, as shown here.

morning and make the request with a CO [correctional officer] breezing by. Joe often overslept and missed his opportunity.[40]

Inmates with mental illness also struggle with transitioning back to society once they are released from prison. When prisoners turn back to the illegal activity that got them arrested in the first place, it is called recidivism. One study found that parolees with mental illness are 36 percent more likely to violate the terms of their parole, causing them to go back to prison. Numerous studies suggest that reentry programs specifically made for people with mental illness— particularly ones built around teams of experts that include mental health providers and social workers— can help reduce this percentage.

Gionfriddo stated that many young people with mental illness also have to deal with being punished rather than given proper care. He said, "If we had full funding for special education services, then we'd identify kids much earlier in the disease process because half of all mental illnesses emerge by the age of 14 … Instead of ignoring kids or suspending or expelling them, we'd actually be able to identify them and treat them."[41]

Following a deadly school shooting in Parkland, Florida, in February 2018, President Donald Trump vowed to tackle the issue of mental health in America, signing a two-year funding bill that set aside $6 billion to address opioid addiction and mental health care. This number was increased to $13 billion several days later. However, the same funding bill also proposed severe cuts to Medicaid, which experts say could have terrible effects on the country's mental health care system.

Trump also proposed opening more mental institutions. However, if institutions are not properly funded, they will have the exact same problems they did in the past. Additionally, opening more institutions and making it easier for officials to commit people to them against their will increases the danger that nonviolent people with mental illnesses will be punished.

Experts say better solutions are to increase funding for mental health care institutions that already exist, make it easier for family members to involuntarily commit someone who shows signs of violence, decrease the stigma surrounding mental illness so more people seek help on their own, and pass stricter gun control laws to decrease the chance that a violent person with a mental illness will be able to buy a gun. Community-based care is less expensive and more humane in the long run than sending people to a mental institution.

Whether the United States will find a solution to humanely care for the country's growing population of people who are mentally ill remains to be seen. As history has shown, without proper funding and resources, any well-meaning solution can turn from highly effective treatment to a living nightmare for the patients who must rely on this care.

Fortunately, modern society seems much more understanding of the challenges people with mental illness face, compared to society during Dorothea Dix's time. Though stigma still exists, recent efforts to combat that stigma and promote transparency and an open dialogue about mental health have gathered much support. Celebrities such as Demi Lovato, Gina Rodriguez, Kristen Bell, Dwayne "The Rock" Johnson, Troian Bellisario, and Ryan Reynolds have all publicly discussed their mental health struggles, helping to fight the idea that mental illness is something shameful to be kept secret. As the culture continues to shift toward understanding and inclusivity, many hope that mental health stigma will become a thing of the past.

Self-Care Is the Best Care

Before an airplane takes off, a flight attendant explains to the passengers all the safety features and instructions. If the cabin pressure drops, they say, oxygen

Ways to Be Supportive

Having a solid support system of family and friends can be immensely helpful for people with schizophrenia. One of the most important ways to help a friend or family member with the disorder is to just be there for them, being a source of comfort, kindness, and understanding. As a young woman with schizophrenia wrote, "Schizophrenia is a lonely disease, and not too many people talk about it (unless it has to do with a crime) and people definitely aren't turning their social media a certain color to raise awareness. Most people with schizophrenia suffer alone, or with their family (if they are lucky enough to have family)."[1]

It is also important for friends and family of someone with a mental illness to maintain their own mental health. The healthier they are, the more energy they have for solving problems and offering encouragement. Then, they feel able to offer practical support, such as the following:

- Do research to learn about mental illness in general and a loved one's case in particular.

- Ask questions about a loved one's treatment plan, and encourage discussion.

- Support the person as they follow their treatment plan; cheer their successes, and offer encouragment when they struggle.

- Listen when a loved one speaks about their mental illness. Do not brush them off or offer unasked-for advice.

- Return to normal life instead of letting life revolve around the person's illness.

- Join a support group for friends and family of people with schizophrenia.

- Make safety a priority and work with the person who has schizophrenia to create a crisis plan in case they slip back into psychosis.

- Remember that recovery is a process, and even though some days will be better than others, that does not mean people should stop trying.

1. Rebecca Chamaa, "What Does Schizophrenia Feel Like?," *A Journey With You: Surviving Schizophrenia*, October 24, 2015. ajourneywithyou.com/2015/10/24/what-does-schizophrenia-look-like/.

masks will automatically drop from overhead to help each passenger breathe. However, they say someone should always put on their own oxygen mask before helping others; it is difficult to help someone else without being able to breathe properly.

This is good advice not just for air travel, but also for life. It is hard to take care of someone who is struggling when the caregiver is tired, is stressed out, and can hardly breathe. That is where self-care comes in handy. Self-care describes things a person does for themselves, deliberately and by choice, to ensure their own mental and physical well-being. Many people are familiar with self-care as something nice someone does as a treat for themselves, such as taking a bubble bath, reading a book, or getting a manicure. However, it also includes making a point to do things that help keep a person's body running well, such as eating a healthy diet, exercising regularly, and getting enough sleep every night. Self-care is incredibly important for every human being, and it is especially important for those who are responsible for the care of others. That added stress can take a toll on a person's mental and physical health, so experts tell caregivers to do what they need to do to take care of themselves, too. It is not selfish or pointless; it is an important part of being an effective helper.

Some additional ideas for self-care include:

- **sweat it out:** The Centers for Disease Control and Prevention (CDC) recommends 2.5 hours of moderate activity every week for adults and 60 minutes of moderate or vigorous activity three times a week for young adults. This could involve walking, running, swimming, riding a bike—whatever works best for the individual. Physical exercise has been proven to improve mental health.

- **unplug for an hour:** Technology can be a fun distraction, but it can also be draining. Taking a break

Self-care, such as getting a massage, can help reduce stress, which generally makes people feel better emotionally and physically equipped to care for a loved one with mental illness.

from social media, television, and everything else can be refreshing.

- **take a nap:** Even a quick snooze can help when someone is extremely tired. Experts say 20 minutes is a good amount of time to nap, as this relieves tiredness without throwing off a person's sleep schedule by making them unable to sleep at night.

- **make time for a fun activity:** Whether it is a visit to a favorite museum, a movie, or even just a stroll through the park, making time for things the person really enjoys is a good way to relieve stress and boost mood.

- **buy a treat:** Whether it is an item of clothing, a special meal, or a new gadget, buying something nice once in a while—and when a person can afford to do so—can make someone feel good.

- **be still:** Many people find that some form of meditation relieves their stress, and studies have shown that it causes changes in the brain that make people stay relaxed longer.

Mental illness, just like physical illness, can be painful and difficult to manage. The negative stigma and internalized shame that often accompany a diagnosis of mental illness can make the situation especially difficult for the individual. However, it is important to remember that a mental illness, just like a physical illness, does not define a person. Humans are complex beings with many facets. Illness is only one aspect among many others that make a person their unique self.

Although schizophrenia is a serious health condition that can impact many aspects of a person's life, it is treatable. With the right support and treatment plan, people with schizophrenia can lead rich, full lives. Their treatment plan may need to be adjusted from time to time to meet their changing needs, and there is nothing wrong with that. What is important is that the person understands their illness and has the care and support they need to live their life fully. Recovery is possible, and every person deserves a chance to live their best life.

NOTES

Introduction: What Is Schizophrenia?

1. "ISSTD Statement on 'Split,'" International Society for the Study of Trauma and Dissociation, accessed on June 26, 2018. www.isst-d.org/downloads/Statement%20on%20Split-final.pdf.

2. "ISSTD Statement on 'Split,'" International Society for the Study of Trauma and Dissociation.

3. Daniel Smith, "This is What Developing Acute Schizophrenia Feels Like," Vice, October 15, 2014. www.vice.com/en_us/article/3b7yvv/this-is-what-developing-acute-schizophrenia-is-like-009.

4. Quoted in Jordyn Taylor, "If You Care About Mental Illness, It's Time to Stop Saying 'Crazy' and 'Insane,'" Mic, June 24, 2016. mic.com/articles/146806/stop-saying-crazy-and-insane-if-you-care-about-mental-illness#.UKRhq2Ar2.

5. Smith, "This is What Developing Acute Schizophrenia Feels Like."

Chapter One: A "Mad" History

6. "Divine Madness—a History of Schizophrenia," History Cooperative, accessed on June 26, 2018. historycooperative.org/divine-madness-a-history-of-schizophrenia/.

7. Ron Powers, *No One Cares About Crazy People: My Family and the Heartbreak of Mental Illness in America*. New York, NY: Hachette Books, 2017, e-book.

8. Amanda Ruggeri, "How Bedlam Became 'a Palace for Lunatics,'" BBC Culture, December 15, 2016. www.bbc.com/culture/story/20161213-how-bedlam-became-a-palace-for-lunatics.

9. "Moral Treatment," Brought to Life, accessed on February 24, 2018. broughttolife.science-museum.org.uk/broughttolife/techniques/moraltreatment.

10. "Schizophrenia: A Brief History," Living with Schizophrenia, accessed on February 24, 2018. www.livingwithschizophreniauk.org/advice-sheets/schizophrenia-a-brief-history/.

11. Quoted in Eileen Buckley, "Recalling Treatment at Buffalo's Former Mental Institution," WBFO, June 5, 2018. news.wbfo.org/post/recalling-treatment-buffalo-s-former-mental-institution.

12. Quoted in Laura Barcella, "How Carrie Fisher Championed Mental Health," *Rolling Stone,* December 28, 2016. www.rollingstone.com/culture/how-carrie-fisher-championed-mental-health-w458009.

13. "Eugenics: Three Generations, No Imbeciles: Virginia, Eugenics, & *Buck v. Bell*," University of Virginia—Claude Moore Health Sciences Library, 2004. exhibits.hsl.virginia.edu/eugenics/3-buckvbell/.

14. Quoted in Philip K. Wilson, "Eugenics," *Encyclopedia Britannica*, accessed on June 27, 2018. www.britannica.com/science/eugenics-genetics.

15. Quoted in Buckley, "Recalling Treatment."

Chapter Two: The Diagnostic Process

16. Quoted in Christopher Lane, "How Schizophrenia Became a Black Disease: An Interview with Jonathan Metzl," *Psychology Today*, May 5, 2010. www.psychologytoday.com/us/blog/side-effects/201005/how-schizophrenia-became-black-disease-interview-jonathan-metzl.

17. Quoted in Lane, "How Schizophrenia Became a Black Disease."

18. Dr. Melissa Heffler, interview by author, March 13, 2018.

19. "DSM-5 Frequently Asked Questions," American Psychiatric Association, accessed on March 4, 2018. www.psychiatry.org/psychiatrists/practice/dsm/feedback-and-questions/frequently-asked-questions.

20. Heffler, interview.

21. Heffler, interview.

Chapter Three: The Biology of Schizophrenia

22. Quoted in "Scientists Discover Neurochemical Imbalance in Schizophrenia," UC San Diego Health, September 11, 2014. health.ucsd.edu/news/releases/Pages/2014-09-11-nuerochemical-imbalance-identified-schizophrenia.aspx.

23. Quoted in Merrit Kennedy, "Major Neurological Conditions Have More in Common Than We Thought, Study Finds," NPR, February 8, 2018. www.npr.org/sections/thetwo-way/2018/02/08/584330475/major-

psychiatric-disorders-have-more-in-common-than-we-thought-study-finds.

24. Adam Piore, "Immune System Offers Major Clue to Schizophrenia," *MIT Technology Review*, January 27, 2016. www.technologyreview.com/s/546136/immune-system-offers-major-clue-to-schizophrenia/.

25. Powers, *No One Cares About Crazy People*, e-book.

26. Quoted in Sharon Begley, "Obama's BRAIN Initiative Yields First Study Results," Reuters, April 30, 2015. www.reuters.com/article/us-science-robomouse/obamas-brain-initiative-yields-first-study-results-idUSKBN-0NL23R20150430.

Chapter Four: Treating Schizophrenia

27. Danielle Miller, "4 Ways Teens Can Access Therapy without Health Insurance," NAMI, June 6, 2018. www.nami.org/Blogs/NAMI-Blog/June-2018/4-Ways-Teens-Can-Access-Therapy-Without-Health-Ins.

28. Miller, "4 Ways Teens Can Access Therapy."

29. Michael T. Compton and Beth Broussard, *The First Episode of Psychosis: A Guide for Patients and Their Families*. New York, NY: Oxford University Press, 2009, p. 87.

30. Heffler, interview.

31. Heffler, interview.

32. Heffler, interview.

33. "Schizophrenia," Mayo Clinic, accessed on July 2, 2018. www.mayoclinic.org/diseases-conditions/schizophrenia/diagnosis-treatment/drc-20354449.

34. "Schizophrenia," NAMI, accessed on July 2, 2018. www.nami.org/Learn-More/Mental-Health-Conditions/Schizophrenia/Support.

35. "Schizophrenia," NAMI.

36. Andrew Wiese, "Accepting My Schizophrenia Diagnosis," NAMI, accessed on June 12, 2018. www.nami.org/Personal-Stories/Accepting-My-Schizophrenia-Diagnosis#.

37. Marie Barse, "Some Schizophrenia Patients Can Cope Without Medication," ScienceNordic, July 23, 2017. sciencenordic.com/some-schizophrenia-patients-can-cope-without-medication.

Chapter Five: Living with Mental Illness

38. Quoted in Sarah Varney, "By the Numbers: Mental Illness Behind Bars," PBS *NewsHour*, May 15, 2014. www.pbs.org/newshour/health/numbers-mental-illness-behind-bars.

39. Quoted in Cathy Cassata, "Is President Trump Right? Should We Open More Mental Institutions?," Healthline, March 6, 2018. www.healthline.com/health-news/president-trump-should-we-open-more-mental-institutions#1.

40. John L. Lennon, "Inside Attica Correctional Facility and How Prisons Deal With Mental Health," *Esquire*, June 5, 2018. www.esquire.com/lifestyle/a20717313/mental-illness-treatment-in-prison/.

41. Quoted in Cassata, "Is President Trump Right? Should We Open More Mental Institutions?"

anosognosia: A symptom of mental illness that makes it difficult for the patient to understand that they have a mental illness.

asylum: An institution that provides care and protection to individuals who need it, such as those who are poor or mentally ill.

cognitive behavioral therapy (CBT): A form of psychotherapy that treats problems and boosts happiness by identifying and changing dysfunctional emotions, behaviors, and thoughts.

delusion: A persistent, false belief regarding the self, other persons, or objects outside the self that is maintained despite indisputable evidence to the contrary.

dopamine: A neurotransmitter that helps control the brain's reward and pleasure centers as well as regulate movement and emotional responses.

electroconvulsive therapy (ECT): Medical treatment involving electric currents being sent to the brain to generate a seizure.

gene: The part of a DNA molecule that passes hereditary information from parents to their offspring.

hallucination: The awareness of something that seems to be experienced through one of the senses but is not real and cannot be sensed by someone else.

lobotomy: The surgical cutting of nerve fibers connecting the brain's frontal lobes to the thalamus that has been performed especially to treat mental illness.

neurologist: A doctor who specializes in treating disorders of the nervous system.

neuron: A nerve cell.

neurotransmitter: A brain chemical that allows neurons to communicate.

psychosis: A serious mental illness marked by the loss of, or greatly lessened, ability to test whether what one is thinking and feeling about the real world is true.

side effect: A secondary, generally unwanted effect of a drug.

ORGANIZATIONS TO CONTACT

American Psychiatric Association (APA)
800 Maine Avenue SW, Suite 900
Washington, DC 20024
(202) 559-3900
www.psychiatry.org
The APA is an organization of psychiatrists working together to ensure humane care and effective treatment for everyone with mental illness. The website includes a directory of psychiatrists by zip code.

Crisis Text Line
741741
www.crisistextline.org
The Crisis Text Line offers free support for those in crisis, 24 hours a day, 7 days a week. Text 741741 from anywhere in the United States to text with a trained Crisis Counselor.

National Alliance on Mental Health (NAMI)
3803 N. Fairfax Drive, Suite 100
Arlington, VA 22203
(800) 950-6264
www.nami.org
NAMI is the nation's largest grassroots mental health organization dedicated to building better lives for the millions of Americans affected by mental illness.

National Institute of Mental Health (NIMH)

Office of Science Policy, Planning, and
Communications
6001 Executive Boulevard, Room 6200, MSC 9663
Bethesda, MD 20892
(866) 615-6464
www.nimh.nih.gov/index.shtml
NIMH is the leading federal agency for research on
mental disorders.

Substance Abuse and Mental Health Services Administration (SAMHSA)

5600 Fishers Lane
Rockville, MD 20857
(877) 726-4727
www.samhsa.gov
This government-run organization leads efforts to
improve public health policy surrounding addiction and
mental illness. Its website provides information on
these topics.

FOR MORE INFORMATION

Books

Abramovitz, Melissa. *What Is Schizophrenia?* San Diego, CA: ReferencePoint Press, 2015.
The author discusses symptoms, causes, and treatment of schizophrenia.

Baldwin, Marjorie L. *Beyond Schizophrenia: Living and Working with a Serious Mental Illness.* Lanham, MD: Rowman & Littlefield Publishers, 2016.
This book explores social and workplace factors that affect employment outcomes for people with schizophrenia (or other serious mental illnesses) and offers recommendations designed to improve employment outcomes for this population.

Powers, Ron. *No One Cares About Crazy People: My Family and the Heartbreak of Mental Health in America.* New York, NY: Hachette Book Group, 2017.
Written by the father of two people with schizophrenia, Powers's book blends the social history of mental illness in America, the public policies that affect the country today, and his personal story of his sons' battles with schizophrenia.

Torrey, E. Fuller. *Surviving Schizophrenia, 6th Edition: A Family Manual.* New York, NY: Harper Perennial, 2013.
This book describes the causes, symptoms, treatment, and course of schizophrenia and also explores living with it from both the patient's and their family's point of view.

Websites

MentalHealth.gov
www.mentalhealth.gov
This government-run website provides information about various mental illnesses, including how to get help.

OK2TALK
ok2talk.org
On this website, which is a project of NAMI, young adults who are struggling with mental health conditions can find a safe place to talk about what they are experiencing by sharing their personal stories of recovery, tragedy, struggle, or hope. Anyone can make a post, and others can "like" it to show support. The website includes a hotline people can call if they want to talk to a trained listener. When sharing personal stories online, it is a good idea not to include identifying or contact information such as school name, home address, or phone number.

OptionB
optionb.org
OptionB is an online organization that helps people cope with adversity and build resiliency through sharing stories, connecting with others in similar situations, providing information on coping strategies, and more. Ask a parent or guardian before joining a support group.

Schizophrenia and Related Disorders Alliance of America (SARDAA)
sardaa.org
This organization was created in 2008 to help improve the lives of people with schizophrenia. The website offers information about support groups, events, the latest research, legal issues that concern people with schizophrenia, and more. SARDAA has also created an app called Health Storylines that helps people with schizophrenia identify patterns in their symptoms and remember to take their medication.

D

E

R

S

ABOUT THE AUTHOR

Michelle Harris was born and raised in Los Angeles, California. She studied at the University of California at Santa Barbara, where she received a Bachelor of Arts degree in psychology in 2008. She has worked as a digital content producer for several years, writing informational and marketing copy for television, online news, and consumer goods. She currently resides in Western New York with her beloved dog, Zoey.